enpa
nal la
nsable
cog fear
sistance
n choose
love
chool

LINCHPIN

LINCHPIN

ARE YOU INDISPENSABLE?

Seth Godin

Illustrations by Jessica Hagy and Hugh MacLeod

PORTFOLIO

PORTFOLIO

Published by the Penguin Group

Penguin Group (USA) Inc., 375 Hudson Street, New York, New York 10014, U.S.A. • Penguin Group (Canada), 90 Eglinton Avenue East, Suite 700, Toronto, Ontario, Canada M4P 2Y3 (a division of Pearson Penguin Canada Inc.) • Penguin Books Ltd, 80 Strand, London WC2R 0RL, England • Penguin Ireland, 25 St. Stephen's Green, Dublin 2, Ireland (a division of Penguin Books Ltd) • Penguin Books Australia Ltd, 250 Camberwell Road, Camberwell, Victoria 3124, Australia (a division of Pearson Australia Group Pty Ltd) • Penguin Books India Pvt Ltd, 11 Community Centre, Panchsheel Park, New Delhi – 110 017, India • Penguin Group (NZ), 67 Apollo Drive, Rosedale, North Shore 0632, New Zealand (a division of Pearson New Zealand Ltd) • Penguin Books (South Africa) (Pty) Ltd, 24 Sturdee Avenue, Rosebank, Johannesburg 2196, South Africa

Penguin Books Ltd, Registered Offices: 80 Strand, London WC2R 0RL, England

First published in 2010 by Portfolio, a member of Penguin Group (USA) Inc.

10 9 8 7 6 5 4 3 2 1

Chart on page 62 by the author. Illustration on page 232 by Hugh MacLeod. All other illustrations by Jessica Hagy.

Library of Congress Cataloging-in-Publication Data
Godin, Seth.
    Linchpin : are you indispensable? / Seth Godin ; illustrations by Jessica Hagy and Hugh MacLeod.
        p.   cm.
    ISBN 978-1-59184-316-0
    ISBN 978-1-59184-327-6 (export edition)
    1. Employee motivation.   2. Employees—Attitudes.   3. Creative thinking.
4. Value added.   5. Work—Psychological aspects.   I. Title.
    HF5549.5.M63.G63 2010
    650.1—dc22   2009036957

Printed in the United States of America
Set in Janson Text with Berthold Akzidenz Grotesk
Designed by Daniel Lagin

for Helene

CONTENTS

A FIRST LOOK AT *LINCHPIN*

The world has changed (again) and the stakes are higher than ever. Now we're facing a full-fledged revolution—a hypercompetitive world involving art and gifts and fear and the ability for you (for anyone) to make an indispensable contribution to something you care about. If you're not indispensable (yet) it's because you haven't made that choice. My goal is to help you see that the choice is yours.

You are not a faceless cog in the machinery of capitalism (anymore). You now have a choice. This book outlines the two paths available to each of us, and teaches you about why you might be resisting the less-traveled (but better) choice.

We have gone from two teams (management and labor) to a third team, the linchpins. These are people who own their own means of production, who can make a difference, lead us, and connect us. The death of the factory means that the entire system we have built our lives around is now upside down. This is either a huge opportunity or a giant threat. Revolutions are frightening because the new benefits sometimes lag behind the old pain. This time, the opportunity is to bring your best self to the marketplace and be rewarded for it.

And it is a choice. A choice to buy into the fear and the system or to chart your own path and create value as you do. It's your job to figure out how to chart the path, because charting the path is the point.

The scam is that just about everything you were taught in school and by the media was an invented myth, a fable designed to prep you to be a compliant worker in the local factory. School exists for a reason, but that reason might not be what you think it is.

The linchpin is an individual who can walk into chaos and create order, someone who can invent, connect, create, and make things happen. Every worthwhile institution has indispensable people who make differences like these.

To become indispensable involves doing difficult work. Labor in the best sense of the word. The act of bringing your whole self to work, of engaging in tasks that require maturity and soul and personal strength, and doing it for the right reason. Linchpins are geniuses, artists, and givers of gifts. They bring humanity to the work, they don't leave it at home. The hard work isn't lifting or shoving or sharpening. The hard work is being brave enough to make a difference.

The Resistance

So, why is this so hard? It turns out that it's biological. Deep within your brain lies the amygdala, the lizard brain. It sets out to sabotage anything that feels threatening, risky, or generous. Until you name, recognize, and deal with the resistance, you will stay frustrated.

The Powerful Culture of Gifts

Art is a gift. A real gift, not part of a deal, not a transaction entered into with reciprocity in mind. The culture of gifts has a long history on this planet, and understanding how it brings people together is a critical step in becoming indispensable.

There Is No Map

Indispensable linchpins are not waiting for instructions, but instead, figuring out what to do next. If you have a job where someone tells you what to do next, you've just given up the chance to create value.

Making the Choice

If value is created by what you choose to do (as opposed to what you were born with), then the essence of becoming a linchpin is a choice. Deciding to overcome the anxiety (false fear) associated with leading and connecting is the choice that few are willing to make.

The Culture of Connection

Linchpins don't work in a vacuum. Your personality and attitude are more important than the actual work product you create, because indispensable work is work that is connected to others.

The Seven Abilities of the Linchpin

What does it take to be indispensable, the person they can't live without?

When It Doesn't Work

There are no guarantees that the marketplace (commerce) will embrace your ideas (art). And when the connection isn't made, blind persistence isn't always the best approach.

Summary

Today is a turning point, a once-in-a-lifetime moment in time when you get to make a choice. Every day, people like you are choosing to go down a less well-defined path, one in which they make choices and make a difference. It turns out that not only does this fulfill our potential as workers and citizens, it is also precisely what the marketplace demands. Instead of focusing on complying with management as a long-term strategy for getting more stuff and being more secure, we have a chance to describe a powerful vision for our future and to actually make it happen. This new dream isn't about obedience, it's about vision and engagement.

Acknowledgments

Bibliography

INTRODUCTION

You Are a Genius

If a genius is someone with exceptional abilities and the insight to find the not so obvious solution to a problem, you don't need to win a Nobel Prize to be one. A genius looks at something that others are stuck on and gets the world unstuck.

So the question is: Have you ever done that?

Have you ever found a shortcut that others couldn't find?

Solved a problem that confounded your family?

Seen a way to make something work that wasn't working before?

Made a personal connection with someone who was out of reach to everyone else?

Even once?

No one is a genius all the time. Einstein had trouble finding his house when he walked home from work every day. But all of us are geniuses sometimes.

The tragedy is that society (your school, your boss, your government, your family) keeps drumming the genius part out. The problem is that our culture has engaged in a Faustian bargain, in which we trade our genius and artistry for apparent stability.

Reality

A guy is riding in the first-class cabin of a train in Spain and to his delight, he notices that he's sitting next to Pablo Picasso. Gathering up his courage, he turns to the master and says, "Señor Picasso, you are a great artist, but why is all your art, all modern art, so screwed up? Why don't you paint reality instead of these distortions?"

Picasso hesitates for a moment and asks, "So what do you think reality looks like?"

The man grabs his wallet and pulls out a picture of his wife. "Here, like this. It's my wife."

Picasso takes the photograph, looks at it, and grins. "Really? She's very small. And flat, too."

This book is about love and art and change and fear. It's about overcoming a multigenerational conspiracy designed to sap your creativity and restlessness. It's about leading and making a difference and it's about succeeding. I couldn't have written this book ten years ago, because ten years ago, our economy wanted you to fit in, it paid you well to fit in, and it took care of you if you fit in. Now, like it or not, the world wants something different from you. We need to think hard about what reality looks like now.

What if you could learn a different way of seeing, a different way of giving, a different way of making a living? And what if you could do that without leaving your job?

This is not a book for the wild-haired crazies your company keeps in a corner. It's a book for you, your boss, and your employees, because the best future available to us is a future where you contribute your true self and your best work. Are you up for that?

One promise: the world to come (and this book) is neither small nor flat.

This Time It's Personal

This is a personal manifesto, a plea from me to you. Right now, I'm not focused on the external, on the tactics organizations use to make great products or spread important ideas. This book is different. It's about a choice and it's about your life. This choice doesn't require you to quit your job, though it challenges you to rethink how you do your job.

The system we grew up with is a mess. It's falling apart at the seams and a lot of people I care about are in pain because the things we thought would work don't. Every day I meet people who have so much to give but have been bullied enough or frightened enough to hold it back. They have become victims, pawns in a senseless system that uses them up and undervalues them.

It's time to stop complying with the system and draw your own map.

Stop settling for what's good enough and start creating art that matters. Stop asking what's in it for you and start giving gifts that change people. Then, and only then, will you have achieved your potential.

For hundreds of years, the population has been seduced, scammed, and brainwashed into fitting in, following instructions, and exchanging a day's work for a day's pay. That era has come to an end and just in time.

You have brilliance in you, your contribution is valuable, and the art you create is precious. Only you can do it, and you must. I'm hoping you'll stand up and choose to make a difference.

Making the Choice

My goal is to persuade you that there is an opportunity available to you, a chance to significantly change your life for the better. Not by doing something that's easy or that you've been trained to do, but by understanding how the rules of our world have fundamentally changed and by taking advantage of this moment to become someone the world believes is indispensable.

It starts by making a simple choice.

I know that you can do this and I hope you will. And once you do, if you do, I'm hoping you'll share the idea with someone you care about.

The Take-Care-of-You Bargain

Here's the deal our parents signed us up for:

Our world is filled with factories. Factories that make widgets and insurance and Web sites, factories that make movies and take care of sick people and answer the telephone. These factories need workers.

If you learn how to be one of these workers, if you pay attention in school, follow instructions, show up on time, and try hard, we will take care of you. You won't have to be brilliant or creative or take big risks.

We will pay you a lot of money, give you health insurance, and offer you job security. We will cherish you, or at the very least, take care of you.

It's a pretty seductive bargain.

So seductive that for a century, we embraced it. We set up our schools and our systems and our government to support the bargain.

It worked. The *Fortune* 500 took care of us. The teachers' union took care of us. The post office and the local retailer took care of us. We followed the instructions, we washed the bottles, we showed up on time, and in return, we got what we needed. It was the American Dream. For a long time, it worked.

But in the face of competition and technology, the bargain has fallen apart.

Job growth is flat at best.

Wages in many industries are in a negative cycle.

The middle class is under siege like never before, and the future appears dismal. People are no longer being taken care of—pensions are gone; 401(k)s have been sliced in half; and it's hard to see where to go from here. You might be the hardworking secretary, the one with institutional knowledge, the person who has given so much and deserves security and respect. And while you might deserve these things, your tenure is no guarantee that you're going to get them.

Suddenly, quite suddenly in the scheme of things, it seems like the obedient worker bought into a sucker's deal. The educated, hardworking masses are still doing what they're told, but they're no longer getting what they deserve.

This situation presents a wonderful opportunity.

Yes, it's an opportunity. An opportunity to actually enjoy what you do, to make a difference to your colleagues and your customers, and to unlock the genius you've been hiding all these years.

It's futile to work hard at restoring the take-care-of-you bargain. The bargain is gone, and it's not worth whining about and it's not effective to complain. There's a new bargain now, one that leverages talent and creativity and art more than it rewards obedience.

Where Does Success Come From?

Every day, bosses, customers, and investors make hard choices about whom to support and whom to eliminate, downsize, or avoid.

For the last twenty years, I've been studying eighteen varieties of that simple question. Some variations:

Why do some tactics work better than others? Why are some employees so much more productive than others? Why do some organizations wilt and fade in the face of a tumultuous market while others thrive? How come some ideas spread far and wide and others are ignored?

This book is my answer to that question.

Where Does Average Come From?

It comes from two places:

1. You have been brainwashed by school and by the system into believing that your job is to do your job and follow instructions. It's not, not anymore.

2. Everyone has a little voice inside of their head that's angry and afraid. That voice is the resistance—your lizard brain—and it wants you to be average (and safe).

If you're not doing as well as you hoped, perhaps it's because the rules of the game were changed, and no one told you.

The rules were written just over two hundred years ago; they worked for a long time, but no longer. It might take you more than a few minutes to learn the new rules, but it's worth it.

Developing Indispensability

You weren't born to be a cog in the giant industrial machine. You were *trained* to become a cog.

There's an alternative available to you. Becoming a linchpin is a stepwise process, a path in which you develop the attributes that make you indispensable. You can train yourself to matter. The first step is the most difficult, the step where you acknowledge that this is a skill, and like all skills, you can (and will) get better at it. Every day, if you focus on the gifts, art, and connections that characterize the linchpin, you'll become a little more indispensable.

> *Do not internalize the industrial model.* You are not one of the myriad of interchangeable pieces, but a unique human being, and if you've got something to say, *say* it, and think well of yourself while you're learning to say it better.
>
> **—David Mamet**

THE NEW WORLD OF WORK

We Are Surrounded by Bureaucrats, Note Takers, Literalists, Manual Readers, TGIF Laborers, Map Followers, and Fearful Employees

The problem is that the bureaucrats, note takers, literalists, manual readers, TGIF laborers, map followers, and fearful employees are in pain. They're in pain because they're overlooked, underpaid, laid off, and stressed out.

The first chapter of Adam Smith's *Wealth of Nations* makes it clear that the way for businesses to win is to break the production of goods into tiny tasks, tasks that can be undertaken by low-paid people following simple instructions. Smith writes about how incredibly efficient a pin-making factory is compared to a few pin artisans making pins by hand. Why hire a supertalented pin maker when ten barely trained pin-making factory workers using a machine and working together can produce a *thousand* times more pins, more quickly, than one talented person working alone can?

For nearly three hundred years, that was the way work worked. What factory owners want is compliant, low-paid, replaceable cogs to run their efficient machines. Factories created productivity, and productivity produced profits. It was fun while it lasted (for the factory owners).

Our society is struggling because during times of change, the very last people you need on your team are well-paid bureaucrats, note takers, literalists, manual readers, TGIF laborers, map followers, and fearful employees. The compliant masses don't help so much when you don't know what to do next.

What we want, what we need, what we must have are indispensable human beings. We need original thinkers, provocateurs, and people who care. We need marketers who can lead, salespeople able to risk making a human connection, passionate change makers willing to be shunned if it is necessary for them to make a point. Every organization needs a linchpin, the one person who can bring it together and make a difference. Some organizations haven't realized this yet, or haven't articulated it, but we need artists.

Artists are people with a genius for finding a new answer, a new connection, or a new way of getting things done.

That would be you.

Where Were You When the World Changed?

I grew up in a world where people did what they were told, followed instructions, found a job, made a living, and that was that.

Now we live in a world where all the joy and profit have been squeezed out of following the rules. Outsourcing and automation and the new marketing punish anyone who is merely good, merely obedient, and merely reliable. It doesn't matter if you're a wedding photographer or an insurance broker; there's no longer a clear path to satisfaction in working for the man.

The factory—that system where organized labor meets patient capital, productivity-improving devices, and leverage—has fallen apart. Ohio and Michigan have lost their "real" factories, just as the factories of the service industries have crumbled as well. Worse still, the type of low-risk, high-stability jobs that three-quarters of us crave have turned into dead-end traps of dissatisfaction and unfair risk.

The essence of the problem: The working middle class is suffering. Wages are stagnant; job security is, for many people, a fading memory; and stress is skyrocketing. Nowhere to run, and apparently, nowhere to hide.

The cause of the suffering is the desire of organizations to turn employees into replaceable cogs in a vast machine. The easier people are to replace, the less they need to be paid. And so far, workers have been complicit in this commoditization.

This is your opportunity. The indispensable employee brings humanity and connection and art to her organization. She is the key player, the one who's difficult to live without, the person you can build something around.

You reject whining about the economy and force yourself to acknowledge that the factory job is dead. Instead, you recognize the opportunity of becoming indispensable, highly sought after, and unique. If a Purple Cow is a product that's worth talking about, the indispensable employee—I call her a linchpin—is a person who's worth finding and keeping.

Thank You for Protecting Us from Our Fear

How was it possible to brainwash billions of people to bury their genius, to give up their dreams, and to buy into the idea of being merely an employee in a factory, following instructions?

Part of it was economic, no doubt about it. Factory work offered average people with small dreams a chance to make a significant change in their standard of living. As a bonus, this new wealth came with a pension, job security, and even health insurance.

But I don't believe that this was enough to explain the massive embrace of a different way of life. The key piece of leverage was this promise: *follow these instructions and you don't have to think.* Do your job and you don't have to be responsible for decisions. Most of all, you don't have to bring your genius to work.

In every corporation in every country in the world, people are waiting to be told what to do. Sure, many of us pretend that we'd love to have control and authority and to bring our humanity to work. But given half a chance, we give it up, in a heartbeat.

Like scared civilians eager to do whatever a despot tells them, we give up our freedoms and responsibilities in exchange for the certainty that comes from being told what to do.

I've seen this in high schools, in Akron, in Bangalore, in London, and in start-ups. People want to be told what to do because they are afraid (petrified) of figuring it out for themselves.

So we take the deal. We agree to do a job in exchange for a set of instructions. And for the hundred years that it led to increasing standards of living, it seemed like a very good deal.

The PERL (Percentage of Easily Replaced Laborers)

In the factory era, the goal was to have the highest PERL. Think about it. If you can easily replace most of your workers, you can pay them less. The less you pay them, the more money you make. The city newspaper, for example, might have four hundred employees, but only a few dozen salespeople and columnists were hard to replace on a moment's notice. The goal was to leverage and defend the system, not the people.

So we built giant organizations (political parties, nonprofits, schools, corporations) filled with easily replaced laborers. Unions fought back precisely because they saw coordinated action as the only way to avoid becoming commodities. Ironically, the work rules they erected merely exacerbated the problem, making every union worker just as good as every other.

The Rule of Ordinary People

One of the most popular books ever written on building a business is called *The E-Myth Revisited*, and here's what its author, Michael E. Gerber, says about the perfect business model:

> ### *The Model Will Be Operated by People with the Lowest Possible Level of Skill*
>
> Yes, I said lowest possible level of skill. Because if your model depends on highly skilled people, it's going to be impossible to replicate. Such people are at a premium in the marketplace. They're also expensive, thus raising the price you will have to charge for your product.

The business model should be such that the employees needed possess the lowest possible level of skill necessary to fulfill the functions for which each is intended. A legal firm ought to have lawyers and a medical firm should hire doctors. But you don't need brilliant lawyers or doctors. What you need is to create the best system through which good lawyers and doctors can be leveraged to produce excellent results.

I can't make this stuff up. His point was that you want a cookie-cutter business that you can scale fast, without regard for finding, nurturing, and retaining linchpin talent. He goes on to coin the "Rule of Ordinary People."

Here's the problem, which you've already guessed. If you make your business possible to replicate, you're not going to be the one to replicate it. Others will. If you build a business filled with rules and procedures that are designed to allow you to hire cheap people, you will have to produce a product without humanity or personalization or connection. Which means that you'll have to lower your prices to compete. Which leads to a race to the bottom.

Indispensable businesses race to the top instead.

Tough Times in Queens

Hector has it rough. Rougher than most.

Every morning, he stands on a street corner in Queens, next to the hardware store and across the street from the Thai restaurant. Hector stands next to his six biggest competitors, waiting for work.

Slowly, a pickup truck pulls up. The contractor behind the wheel is looking for workers, day laborers. He knows that every morning, they'll be on this corner, waiting for him. He rolls down the window and offers minimum wage. Which is a lot for this kind of work.

All the workers seem the same. They're bundled up against the cold, and they're willing to work cheap. So he picks three and drives away.

Hector is left on the corner, in the cold. Maybe someone else will come by today. Maybe not.

He's one of many, a fungible product, a nonchoice. The contractor didn't expend any time or effort on his choice because it didn't really matter. He needed cheap physical labor and he got it. He needed obedient workers able to follow simple instructions, and here they were.

And Hector got nothing. Hector went home, as he often does, with nothing.

Your Street Corner

We don't want Hector's story to resonate with us, because it's disturbing.

Every business is a lot like Hector. Every business stands next to plenty of other businesses, each striving to be like the other, but maybe a little better. Every business waits for the next customer to come along and pick their company.

And of course, sometimes a prospect does pick a particular business. She recognizes it or trusts it or it comes with a recommendation. But more and more (and most of the time), she does precisely what the contractor in Queens did. She picks the cheap one. They're all the same.

And you? Your résumé sits in a stack next to plenty of other résumés, each striving to fit in and meet the requirements. Your cubicle is next to the other cubes, each like the other. Your business card and suit and approach to problems—all designed to fit in. You keep your head down and you work hard and you hope you get picked.

Sounds a lot like Hector. This is uncomfortable, but it's true. The people you're hoping will hire you, buy from you, support you, and interact with you have more choices and less time than ever before.

How Companies (Used to) Make Money

The difference between what an employee is paid and how much value she produces leads to profit. If the worker captures all the value in her salary, there's no profit.

As a result, capitalist profit-maximizing investors have long looked for a way to turn low-wage earners into high-value producers. Give someone who makes five dollars a day an efficient machine, a well-run assembly line, and a detailed manual, and you ought to be able to make five or twenty or a thousand times what you paid in labor.

So, the goal is to hire as many obedient, competent workers, as cheaply as you possibly can. If you can use your productivity advantage to earn five dollars in profit for every dollar you pay in wages, you win. Do it with a million employees and you hit a home run.

The problem?

Someone else is getting better than you at hiring cheap and competent workers. They can ship the work overseas, or buy more machines, or cut corners faster than you can.

The other problem?

Consumers are not loyal to cheap commodities. They crave the unique, the remarkable, and the human. Sure, you can always succeed for a while with the cheapest, but you earn your place in the market with humanity and leadership. It's certainly possible for a shopper to buy food more cheaply than they sell it at Trader Joe's. But Trader's keeps growing, because the combination of engaged employees, cutting-edge products, and fun brings people back. Even people trying to save a buck.

The cheap strategy doesn't scale very well, so the only way to succeed is to add value by amplifying the network and giving workers a platform, not by forcing them to pretend to be machines. The fickle nature of price-shopping consumers is bad news for many companies, the companies that tried to be cheap at all costs, because now they must figure out how to make a profit from expensive, unique, disobedient employees.

Those are the only two choices. Win by being more ordinary, more standard, and cheaper. Or win by being faster, more remarkable, and more human.

A Century of Interchangeable, Disposable Labor

Just over a century ago, leaders of our society started building a system that is now so ingrained, most of us assume that it's always been here and always will be.

We continue to operate as if that system is still here, but every day we do that is a day wasted, dollars lost, an opportunity squandered. And you need to see why.

The system we grew up with is based on a simple formula: Do your job. Show up. Work hard. Listen to the boss. Stick it out. Be part of the system. You'll be rewarded.

That's the scam. Strong words, but true. You've been scammed. You traded years of your life to be part of a giant con in which you are most definitely not the winner.

If you've been playing that game, it's no wonder you're frustrated. That game is over.

There are no longer any great jobs where someone else tells you precisely what to do.

(The Final Straw: The Law of the Mechanical Turk)*

Here's the law: Any project, if broken down into sufficiently small, predictable parts, can be accomplished for awfully close to free.

Jimmy Wales led the tiny team at Wikipedia that destroyed the greatest reference book of all time. And almost all of them worked for free.

The *Encyclopaedia Britannica* was started in 1770 and is maintained by a staff of more than a hundred full-time editors. Over the last 250 years, it has probably cost more than a hundred million dollars to build and edit.

Wikipedia, on the other hand, is many times bigger, far more popular, and significantly more up-to-date, and it was built for almost free. No single person could have done this. No team of a thousand, in fact. But by breaking the development of articles into millions of one-sentence or one-paragraph projects, Wikipedia took advantage of the law of the Mechanical Turk. Instead of relying on a handful of well-paid people

---

* There are several sections throughout that could be considered long footnotes. These are passages you can easily skip without losing the main thread, but I believe they add some interesting historical or scientific context. I tend to find footnotes distracting, so instead I've marked the title of each with (parentheses). Skip or read, up to you.

calling themselves professionals, Wikipedia thrives by using the loosely coordinated work of millions of knowledgeable people, each happy to contribute a tiny slice of the whole.

The original Mechanical Turk was a chess-playing "computer" built in the same year that the *Encyclopaedia Britannica* was founded. Invented by Wolfgang von Kempelen, the Turk wasn't actually a computer at all, but merely a box with a small person hidden inside. A person pretending to be a computer.

Amazon.com took the idea of a man inside the computer and created a service with the same name. A person or company can present a task to the Mechanical Turk Web site, and hordes of invisible people will chip away at it, doing work that's eerily human but requires no personal interaction and very little money. These hardworking people are like the little man inside the chess computer: you can't see them, but they're doing all the work.

For example, John Jantsch took an interview he did with me (about forty minutes of audio) and posted it to a site that uses the Turk as its labor. For just a few dollars, the site took the recording, chopped it into tiny bits, and parceled it out to anonymous laborers who each transcribed their little section. Less than three hours later, it was sewn back together and the typed transcript was delivered to John.

Instead of paying the industry rate of two dollars a minute (about eighty dollars), services like CastingWords do transcription for less than fifty cents a minute using the Turk. They pay their workers (all of whom speak English, know how to type, and have a computer with an Internet connection) about nineteen cents for each minute transcribed. I figure that's about two dollars an hour when you calculate all their labor. And there's no shortage of transcribers. An eighty-dollar project becomes a fifteen-dollar project when you process it with the Mechanical Turk. That's a 70 percent decrease in cost and a vast increase in speed.

The Internet has turned white-collar work into something akin to building a pyramid in Egypt. No one could build the entire thing, but anyone can haul one brick into place.

Here's the scary part: some bosses want their employees (you?) to become the next Mechanical Turk. Is that your dream job?

(The Pursuit of Interchangeability)

In 1765, a French general, Jean-Baptiste Gribeauval, started us down the endless path toward interchangeable parts. He demonstrated that if the French military possessed muskets with parts that could work from one gun to the other, the cost of repairing and even making the guns would drop.

Until then the parts in every device, machine, and weapon were hand fitted together. A screw did not fit any nut but only the one it was made for, a gun trigger would not slot into any other trigger holder but the one it came with, and the barrel would not fit into any other stock except the one it was fitted for. Essentially, every gun was custom made and assembled.

Thomas Jefferson encountered Gribeauval and his acolyte Honorè Blanc in Paris and lobbied hard to bring their ideas back to the United States. When Eli Whitney got an order to produce ten thousand guns for the federal government, a big part of the project was figuring out how to make the parts interchangeable.

For decades, armorers in the Northeast struggled at great cost to develop the technology to produce standardized parts for guns. Other industries were slow to come around. As late as 1885, Singer sewing machines, perhaps the most sophisticated device made in the United States in quantity, were essentially custom-made, each one unable to work with parts from the other.

Henry Ford changed all this. His development (and promotion) of mass production meant that cars could be made in huge quantities and at very low cost. Capitalism had found its holy grail. Within two years of the launch of the Ford System, the productivity at some Ford plants had increased by 400 percent or more.

The essence of mass production is that every part is interchangeable. Time, space, men, motion, money, and material—each was made more efficient because every piece was predictable and separate. Ford's discipline was to avoid short-term gains in exchange for always seeking the interchangeable, always standardizing.

It only follows, then, that as you eliminate the skilled worker, the finisher, the custom-part maker, then you also save money on wages as you build a company that's easy to scale. In other words, *first you have interchangeable parts, then you have interchangeable workers.* By 1925, the die was cast. The goal was to hire the lowest-skilled laborer possible, at the lowest possible wage. To do anything else was financial suicide.

That's the labor market we were trained for.

Was the System Always About Obedience?

Imagine a stack of 400 quarters. Each quarter represents 250 years of human culture, and the entire stack signifies the 100,000 years we've had organized human tribes. Take the top quarter off the stack. This one quarter represents how many years our society has revolved around factories and jobs and the world as we see it. The other 399 coins stand for a very different view of commerce, economy, and culture. Our current view might be the new normal, but the old normal was around for a very long time.

Telling your family that you had a "job" and were moving away to go work in a factory of some sort was unheard of. Five or six generations ago, when it actually started happening, it was a social upheaval of huge proportions. It changed the world.

Having a factory job is not a natural state. It wasn't at the heart of being a human until recently. We've been culturally brainwashed to believe that accepting the hierarchy and lack of responsibility that come with a factory job is the one way, the only way, and the best way.

Art and Initiative and Who's an Artist Now?

I'm sitting next to Zeke on the plane.

Well, I'm sitting but Zeke isn't. Zeke is two. He spends the entire flight standing, walking around, poking, smiling, asking, touching, responding, reacting, testing, and exploring.

Is it possible that you were like Zeke?

What happened?

Somewhere along the way, we baked it out of you. And that's a shame, because what Zeke has (and what so many have lost) is exactly what we need.

We were all hunters.

Then they invented farming, and we became farmers.

And we were all farmers.

Then they invented the factory, and we all became factory workers. Factory workers who followed instructions, supported the system, and got paid what they were worth.

Then the factory fell apart.

And what's left for us to work with? Art.

Now, success means being an artist.

In fact, history is now being written by the artists while the factory workers struggle. The future belongs to chefs, not to cooks or bottle washers. It's easy to buy a cookbook (filled with instructions to follow) but really hard to find a chef book.

The Myth of the White-Collar Job

Most white-collar workers wear white collars, but they're still working in the factory.

They push a pencil or process an application or type on a keyboard instead of operating a drill press. The only grease they have to get off their clothes at the end of the day is the grease from the take-out food at lunch.

But it's factory work.

It's factory work because it's planned, controlled, and measured. It's factory work because you can optimize for productivity. These workers know what they're going to do all day—and it's still morning.

The white-collar job was supposed to save the middle class, because it was machineproof. A machine could replace a guy hauling widgets up a flight of stairs, but a machine could never replace someone answering the phone or running the fax machine.

Of course, machines *have* replaced those workers. Worse, much worse, is that competitive pressures (and greed) have encouraged most organizations to turn their workers into machines.

If we can measure it, we can do it faster.

If we can put it in a manual, we can outsource it.

If we can outsource it, we can get it cheaper.

The end results are legions of frustrated workers, wasted geniuses each and every one of them, working like automatons, racing against the clock to crank out another policy, get through another interaction, see another patient.

It doesn't have to be this way.

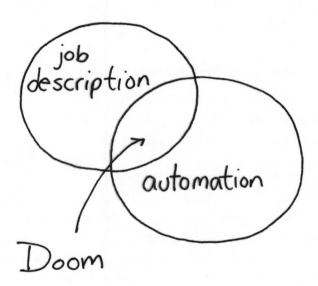

Average Is Over

Our world no longer fairly compensates people who are cogs in a giant machine.

There's stress because for many of us, that's all we know. Schools and society have reinforced this approach for generations.

It turns out that what we need are gifts and connections and humanity—and the artists who create them.

Leaders don't get a map or a set of rules. Living life without a map requires a different attitude. It requires you to be a linchpin.

Linchpins are the essential building blocks of tomorrow's high-value organizations. They don't bring capital or expensive machinery, nor do they blindly follow instructions and merely contribute labor. Linchpins are indispensable, the driving force of our future.

The rest of this book is about changing your posture, and doing it right away.

One last favor before you start: At some point, you may get frustrated and decide to stop reading. Before you do that, I'm begging (begging!) you to read my short chapter, "The Resistance," on page 101. It will explain why you're frustrated.

When the New System Replaces the Old

Revolutions are rare, which is why they always seem to take us by surprise. Electricity was revolutionary. No one had any idea how it would change everything, including the ancient system of domestic labor. A house like yours would have taken half a dozen servants to maintain before electricity.

When electricity showed up in people's homes, it never occurred to builders or electricians that perhaps people would want electrical outlets. Every home with electricity had a few light fixtures and that was it. When the washing machine was introduced, the only way to power it was to unscrew your light bulb and screw in the cord of your washing machine. Hundreds of people a year died using washing machines, because the new system wasn't particularly well organized or understood.

It's hard to describe how significantly different the postindustrial rules are, but I'll try. The good news is that it probably isn't as fatal as a washing machine.

Who Wins?

When John Jantsch uses the Mechanical Turk to get an interview transcribed for 30 percent of the old-school price, it's pretty clear who wins. He does. He keeps the money that would have gone to a well- (or at least fairly well-) paid professional.

And the transcriber who used to make a living at this? He loses.

Over and over again, in every industry, precisely the same calculation takes place. "Should I pay significantly more to have it done the old way, the local way, the traditional way, the way that pays a neighbor a living wage—or should I keep the money?"

In our rush to build, profit, acquire, and otherwise leverage our efforts, we almost always pick the fast and cheap alternative, particularly if it's as good as (or better than) what it replaced.

Do you still use a full-price stockbroker? Odds are that somewhere along the way, you realized you could trade on your own, for close to free.

Does your airline still pay travel agents a 10 percent commission? Odds are that the airline decided to keep that 10 percent (which is greater than the profit on the flight itself), rather than pay someone to use Travelocity while you sat and watched.

Have you chosen to shop at Wal-Mart? There's plenty of research that indicates that every time Wal-Mart enters a community, jobs disappear, businesses close, and the base of the town decays. That's okay, though, because you can get a jar of pickles the size of a Volkswagen for three dollars.

Abstract macroeconomic theories are irrelevant to the people making a million tiny microeconomic decisions every day in a hypercompetitive world. And those decisions repeatedly favor fast and cheap over slow and expensive.

There are pundits who will go to great lengths to persuade you that these decisions are selfish and shortsighted and even morally wrong. Books that will deplore capitalism in all its forms and argue that we need to legislate an alternative.

I don't buy the plausibility or implementability of the argument in favor of freezing things as they were. I think these well-meaning authors have been brainwashed into believing that the old version of the American Dream was a right, and that it was somehow baked into who we are as people.

(You Are What You Do)

Karl Marx and Friedrich Engels wrote, "By producing their means of subsistence men are indirectly producing their actual material life." They went on to argue that what we do all day, the way money is made, drives our schooling, our politics, and our community.

For our entire lives, the push has been to produce, to conform, and to consume.

What will you do if these three pillars change? What happens when the world cares more about unique voices and remarkable insights than it does about cheap labor on the assembly line?

Marx also traced our evolution from a single-class world (tribe members) to a world with two levels: the bourgeoisie and the proletariat.

The bourgeoisie has capital to invest and factories to run. Members of this class own the means of production, giving them considerable power over the workers. The hardworking "proletariat" are indebted to the bourgeoisie because they can't build their own factories. They don't have the capital or the organization to do so.

Makes sense to me. For two centuries or more, the gulf was distinct. You were on one side or the other.

Now, though, the proletariat owns the means of production. Now, the workers are self-organized online. Now, access to capital and the ability to find one another are no longer problems.

If the factories are our minds—if the thing the market values is insight or creativity or engagement—then capital isn't nearly the factor it used to be. There's a third layer to the economy now—call them the linchpins. These are people who are not proles (waiting for instructions and using someone else's machines), nor are they princes or barons of industry. The linchpins leverage something *internal*, not external, to create a position of power and value.

Remember Adam Smith's pin-making machine? Now, each of us owns our own machine, if we choose. Now, each person, working solo or in a team, already possesses the means of production. They are indispensable, if they want to be.

(Karl Marx and Adam Smith Agreed)

Both great social economists said the same thing: There are two teams, management and labor. Management owns the machines, labor follows the rules.

Management wins when it can get the most work for the least pay, and the more controlled the output, the better. Smith thought this was a good thing. Marx saw this as a lousy deal for labor and insisted that the entire structure be forcibly abandoned.

What if there were no longer only two sides? Not just capital versus labor, but a third team, one that straddled elements of both? I think there's a huge opportunity for a third kind of participant, a linchpin, and now there is an opportunity to change all the rules that we've lived with all our lives. There is a shortage of this third kind of worker, and that shortage means that the market needs you desperately. The con game is ending, at least for people passionate enough to do something about it.

The End of ABC and the Search for the Difference Maker

Thornton May correctly points out that we have reached the end of what he calls attendance-based compensation (ABC). There are fewer and fewer good jobs where you can get paid merely for showing up. Instead, successful organizations are paying for people who make a difference and are shedding everyone else.

Just about anyone can be trained to show up. Anyone can unlock the door of the local coffee shop in the morning or monitor the dials at the power plant.

What does it mean to make a difference?

Some jobs are likely to remain poorly paid, low in respect, and high in turnover. These are jobs where attendance (showing up) is all that really matters. Other jobs, the really good jobs, are going to be filled with indispensable people, people who make a difference by doing work that's really hard to find from anyone else.

Owning the Means of Production

This changes everything.

When labor is dependent on management for the factory and the machines and the systems they use to do their work, the relationship is fraught with issues over power and control. The factory needs labor, sure, but labor really needs the factory. It was always easier for management to replace labor than it was for labor to find a new factory.

Today, the means of production = a laptop computer with Internet connectivity. Three thousand dollars buys a worker an entire factory.

This change is a fundamental shift in power and control. When you can master the communication, conceptual, and connectivity elements of the new work, then you have more power than management does. And if management attracts, motivates, and retains great talent, then it has more leverage than the competition.

It starts with bloggers, musicians, writers and others who don't need anyone's support or permission to do their thing. So a blogger named Brian Clark makes a fortune launching a wonderful new theme for Wordpress. And Perez Hilton becomes rich and famous writing on his blog. Abbey Ryan makes almost a hundred thousand dollars a year painting a tiny oil painting each day and selling it on eBay. These individuals have all the technical, manufacturing, and distribution support they need, so they are both capitalists and workers.

The organizations they work for have a very low PERL. In fact, for solely owned organizations, there aren't *any* easily replaced laborers.

This idea is spreading, faster than most of us realize. Now, the thriving organization consists of well-organized linchpins doing their thing in concert, creating more value than any factory ever could. Instead of trying to build organizations filled with human automatons, we've realized we must go the other way.

Mediocrity and the Web

Hugh MacLeod: "The web has made kicking ass easier to achieve, and mediocrity harder to sustain. Mediocrity now howls in protest."

The Internet has raised the bar because it's so easy for word to spread about great stuff. There's more junk than ever before, more lousy writing, more pointless products. But this abundance of trash is overwhelmed by the market's ability to distribute news about the great stuff.

Of course, mediocrity isn't going to go away. Yesterday's remarkable is today's really good and tomorrow's mediocre.

Mediocre is merely a failed attempt to be really good.

The Hierarchy of Value

<pre>
                                          Create/invent
                                  Connect
                          Sell
                   Produce
             Grow
        Hunt
   Lift
</pre>

There are always more people at the bottom of the stairs, doing hard work that's easy to learn. As you travel up the hierarchy, the work gets easier, the pay gets better, and the number of people available to do the work gets smaller.

Lots of people can lift. That's not paying off anymore. A few people can sell. Almost no one puts in the work to create or invent. Up to you.

(How the Average Subsidize the Merely Mediocre— and the Above Average Get Screwed)

Let's say you're the boss, the guy with the map, the person generating jobs and taking profits. You have a business model that allows you to hire people to manipulate data or make sales or do some other task that you can write down in a manual.

An exceptional performer earns you $30 for every hour he works. A good employee is worth $25 an hour, and a mediocre worker can contribute about $20 an hour in profit.

If you can't tell who's mediocre and who's exceptional when you do the hiring, and you want to pay everyone a standard rate, how much should you pay?

Well, other than "as little as possible," the answer is certainly less than $25 an hour. Probably less than $20 an hour. You want every employee to make money, even the mediocre ones.

Which means that all your other employees are getting paid less to make up for the ones who contribute the least. The exceptional performers are getting paid a *lot* less, which is why they should (and will) leave. Exceptional performers are starting to realize that it doesn't pay to do factory work at factory wages only to subsidize the boss.

Remarkable People

In *Purple Cow*, I made a simple argument:

Corporations have no right to our attention. For years (or decades), corporations made average products for average people and routinely interrupted us, hoping we would notice them—and eventually, we stopped paying attention. Now, the only way to grow is to stand out, to create something worth talking about, to treat people with respect and to have them spread the word.

Now I want to make a similar but much more personal argument:

You have no right to that job or that career. After years of being taught that you have to be an average worker for an average organization, that society would support you for sticking it out, you discover that the rules have changed. The only way to succeed is to be remarkable, to be talked about. But when it comes to a person, what do we talk about? People are not products with features, benefits, and viral marketing campaigns; they are individuals. If we're going to talk about them, we're going to discuss what they do, not who they are.

You don't become indispensable merely because you are different. But the only way to be indispensable is to be different. That's because if you're the same, so are plenty of other people.

The only way to get what you're worth is to stand out, to exert emotional labor, to be seen as indispensable, and to produce interactions that organizations and people care deeply about.

THINKING ABOUT YOUR CHOICE

Can You Become Indispensable?

Yes, you can.

This is an important question and it deserves a thoughtful answer.

The first thing to realize is that other people have done this before you. Other people have survived the corporate school system, have survived their first job, have survived a mother-in-law telling them what to do—and have still done the challenging work it takes to become indispensable.

That's essential to know, because that means it's not impossible.

The second thing, even more important than the first, is that the people who have made this transition have nothing on you. Not a thing.

In every case, the linchpins among us are not the ones born with a magical talent. No, they are people who have decided that a new kind of work is important, and trained themselves to do it.

Sure, being tall helps you become a star in basketball, but how many of us have a shot at playing in the NBA? For the rest of us, it's not about what you're born with, it's about what you do.

Teaching Remarkable

Where do the great artists, writers, product developers, copywriters, inventors, scientists, process engineers, and chefs come from?

Explain this: If I make a list of great artists (Alice Waters, Herschell Gordon Lewis, Spike Lee, Eliyahu Goldratt, Muddy Waters, Cory Doctorow, Richard Feynman, Shepard Fairey), not one of the names on this particular list is the product of a school designed to create him or her.

A great school experience won't keep you from being remarkable, but it's usually not sufficient to guarantee that you will become so. There's something else at work here.

Great schools might work; lousy schools definitely stack the deck against you. Why is society working so hard to kill our natural-born artists? When we try to drill and practice someone into subservient obedience, we're stamping out the artist that lives within.

Let me be really clear: Great teachers are wonderful. They change lives. We need them. The problem is that most schools don't like great teachers. They're organized to stamp them out, bore them, bureaucratize them, and make them average.

Why are you working so hard to bury your natural-born instincts? I've never met someone who had no art in them, though it's buried sometimes. Markets are crying out. We need you to stand up and be remarkable. Be human. Contribute. Interact. Take the risk that you might make someone upset with your initiative, innovation, and insight—it turns out that you'll probably delight them instead.

Consumers say that all they want are cheap commodities. Given the choice, though, most of us, most of the time, seek out art. We seek out experiences and products that deliver more value, more connection, and more experience, and change us for the better. You can learn how to do this if you want to.

If You Want . . .

If you want a job where it's okay to follow the rules, don't be surprised if you get a job where following the rules is all you get to do.

If you want a job where the people who work for you do exactly what they're told, don't be surprised if your boss expects precisely the same thing from you.

If you want a job where you don't need to be creative because the company's cost structure is so aggressive that customers just materialize, don't be surprised if the low cost structure costs you your job.

If you want a job where you get to do more than follow instructions, don't be surprised if you get asked to do things they never taught you in school.

If you want a job where you take intellectual risks all day long, don't be surprised if your insights get you promoted.

Limited or Unlimited?

You can see your marketplace as being limited, a zero-sum game, a place where in order for one person to win, another must lose.

Or you can see it as unlimited. A place where talent creates growth and the market increases in size.

Consider Kim Berry, who runs the Programmers Guild, a nonprofit that lobbies Congress to limit or ban H-1B visas for talented computer programmers from overseas. He has said that for every person from India or China who gets a job programming in the United States, someone who was born here loses a job. It's win/lose, in his view, not win/win.

It's very difficult to be generous if you have this point of view. In a zero-sum game, the generous among us are fools, easily taken advantage of.

On the other hand, if you believe that great talent leads to more innovation and more productivity, which then lead to more demand, generosity is the very best strategy. If every great programmer were given the best tools, the best marketing, and the best technology, imagine how much more work that would create for the members of the Programmers Guild. If we enlarged the pie by bringing in the best programmers from around the world, it's inevitable that tons of jobs would be created for local talent as well.

It seems to me that your outlook is completely due to your worldview. If you believe that all programmers are fairly average, then the pie is limited. If you believe that your job is to do your job (follow the map) and go home, then of course it's a zero-sum game.

The linchpin sees the world very differently. Exceptional insight, productivity, and generosity make markets bigger and more efficient. This situation leads to more opportunities and ultimately a payoff for everyone involved. The more you give, the more the market gives back.

Abundance is possible, but only if we can imagine it and then embrace it.

Will You Still Be Loved?

This is a more powerful question, and a difficult one. It's entirely possible that once you choose to become indispensable, you will no longer be loved. Not by the same people who love you now, perhaps, nor for the same reasons.

But (and I know it's a big but) either those people will come around, or they never loved you in the first place, did they?

Special Circumstances

It's easy to argue that this genius stuff is for other people, not you. Those other people have gifts, or genes, or education or background or connections. It's easy to fool yourself into believing that genius works for them, but it won't work for you.

Of course. Except Jeff Bezos and Steve Jobs were raised by adoptive parents, and Nelson Mandela changed the world from a jail cell. Except that Jill Sobule struggled just as much as every other acoustic singer-songwriter but didn't give up. Except that Cathy Hughes dropped out of the University of Nebraska at Omaha and ended up as the first black woman running a public company in the United States. I don't have room to list all the less famous people who had the same resources you do, but were willing to accept the genius label and make a choice.

You Can't?

At the age of four, you were an artist.

And at seven, you were a poet.

And by the time you were twelve, if you had a lemonade stand, you were an entrepreneur.

Of course you can do something that matters. I guess I'm wondering if you *want* to.

There may be a voice in your head that is ready to announce that you can't possibly do what I'm describing. You don't have what it takes; you're not smart enough or trained enough or (sheesh) gifted enough to pull this off.

I'd like to ask for a simple clarification.

You can't—or you don't want to?

I'll accept the second. It's quite possible that you don't want to. It's possible that making this commitment is too scary or too much work. It's possible that it appears too risky to put yourself on the line and make a commitment to becoming indispensable. A commitment like this raises the bar, and for some people, that might be too high.

Perhaps you don't want to because it feels financially irresponsible. I think that's an error in judgment on your part, since becoming a linchpin is in fact the most financially responsible choice you can make. But that's your call, and if you decide you don't want to, fine with me.

But can't?

I don't buy that for a second.

The New American Dream

Do you remember the old American Dream?

It struck a chord with millions of people (in the United States and in the rest of the world, too). Here's how it goes:

> Keep your head down
>
> Follow instructions
>
> Show up on time
>
> Work hard
>
> Suck it up

. . . you will be rewarded. As we've seen, that dream is over.

The new American Dream, though, the one that markets around the world are embracing as fast as they can, is this:

> Be remarkable
>
> Be generous
>
> Create art
>
> Make judgment calls
>
> Connect people and ideas

. . . and we have no choice but to reward you.

What Would Make You Impossibly Good at Your Job?

If your organization wanted to replace you with someone far better at your job than you, what would they look for? I think it's unlikely that they'd seek out someone willing to work more hours, or someone with more industry experience, or someone who could score better on a standardized test.

No, the competitive advantage the marketplace demands is someone more human, connected, and mature. Someone with passion and energy, capable of seeing things as they are and negotiating multiple priorities as she makes useful decisions without angst. Flexible in the face of change, resilient in the face of confusion.

All of these attributes are choices, not talents, and all of them are available to you.

"Not My Job"

Three words can kill an entire organization.

As the world moves faster and engagements become more fluid, the category of "not my job" keeps getting bigger and bigger.

Amazon had a cataloguing glitch on a Friday. Because of an honest mistake, thousands of books with adult homosexual content were banned from their index. Over the weekend, tens of thousands of people blogged and tweeted about "censorship" on Amazon's part. It wasn't until the end of Sunday that the company responded. On the Internet, thirty-six hours is like a month. Why did it take so long? Probably because it was no one's job to monitor the Internet and respond with authority on behalf of Amazon.

The bathroom at New York's Museum of Natural History has insufficient wastepaper bins, so the one that's there is always overflowing. It's the janitor's job to empty the can as often as he can, but who has the job of installing a second can?

In a factory, doing a job that's not yours is dangerous. Now, if you're a linchpin, doing a job that's not getting done is essential.

More Obedience

Would your organization be more successful if your employees were more obedient?

Or, consider for a second: would you be more successful if your employees were more artistic, motivated, connected, aware, passionate, and genuine?

You can't have both, of course.

Would your career advance if you could figure out a way to do an even better job of following your boss's instructions?

Or, just maybe, would you be more successful if you were more artistic, motivated, aware, and genuine?

That's the choice. Your choice.

Secret Memo for Employees

Given the chance, you should choose to be indispensable.

After all, if you're the linchpin, the company *has* to treat you better. Pay you fairly. You won't be the first to be shown the door in a slow period; in fact, you'll be the last.

Not only do you have security, but you also have confidence. The confidence to make a difference in your organization and to do work that matters.

If you can be human at work (not a machine), you'll discover a passion for work you didn't know you had. When work becomes personal, your customers and coworkers are more connected and happier. And that creates even more value.

When you're not a cog in a machine, an easily replaceable commodity, you'll get paid what you're worth. Which is more.

Secret Memo for Employers

You want your employees to be indispensable.

Really? After all, if they're the linchpins, you have to treat them better. Pay them fairly. You won't be able to quickly fire them for any reason, knowing how easy they will be to replace with all those folks lining up at the door. The linchpin represents a threat to the orderly execution of your agenda, because the linchpin is necessary. The linchpin has power!

No one is irreplaceable, of course, because over time someone can be trained to fill the shoes of your linchpin employee. But right now, knowing you have to depend on someone is a scary feeling. Not only does he have power, but he might leave you hanging. This isn't what you were taught in school.

Here's the win (actually, there are two):

First, understand that your competition has been building a faceless machine exactly like yours. And when customers have the choice between faceless options, they pick the cheapest, fastest, more direct option. If you want customers to flock to you, it's tempting to race to the bottom of the price chart. There's not a lot of room for profit there, though. You can't out-Amazon Amazon, can you?

In a world that relentlessly races to the bottom, you lose if you also race to the bottom. The only way to win is to race to the top.

When your organization becomes more human, more remarkable,

faster on its feet, and more likely to connect directly with customers, it becomes indispensable. The very thing that made your employee a linchpin makes YOU a linchpin. An organization of indispensable people doing important work is remarkable, profitable, and indispensable in and of itself.

Second, the people who work for you, the ones you freed to be artists, will rise to a level you can't even imagine. When people realize that they are not a cog in a machine, an easily replaceable commodity, they take the challenge and grow. They produce more than you pay them to, because you are paying them with something worth more than money. They do more than they're paid to, on their own, because they value quality for its own sake, and they want to do good work. They *need* to do good work. Anything less feels intellectually dishonest, and like a waste of time. In exchange, you're giving them freedom, responsibility, and respect, which are priceless.

As a result of these priceless gifts, expect that the linchpins on your staff won't abuse their power. In fact, they'll work harder, stay longer, and produce more than you pay them to. Because everyone is a person, and people crave connection and respect.

This Is No Time for Dumb Tools

The architecture of our systems is set up so that the people at the top know more. The goal is to hire as many cheap but talented people as possible, give them a rule book, and have them follow instructions to the letter.

Go to a McDonald's. Order a Big Mac. Order a chocolate milkshake. Drink half the milkshake.

Eat half the Big Mac.

Put the Big Mac into your milkshake and walk up to the counter.

Say, "I can't drink this milkshake . . . there's a Big Mac in it."

The person at the counter will give you a refund. Why? Because it's easier to give her a rule than it is to hire people with good judgment. The rule is, "When in doubt, give a refund."

Multiply this by millions of jobs at millions of organizations and you see what you end up with: systems everywhere, manuals, rules, and a few people at the top working hard to dream up new ones.

When machines came along, we replicated this process. Teach that robot arm how to spray paint, and have it follow specific rules. Et cetera.

Then something fascinating happened. Kevin Kelly first wrote about this ten years ago: it turns out that GM saves $1.5 million a year by letting the robot arms think for themselves! The more GM enables the swarm of dumb machines to make decisions, bid against each other, network, and interact, the better they work.

The world works too fast for centralized control. These systems can't be run by a supervisor at the top of the organizational chart.

Bullet trains in Japan run fast and on schedule without a centralized switchboard. It turns out that pushing decision making down the chart is faster and more efficient.

So now, having learned from machines, organizations are applying the same logic to people. Letting people in the organization use their best judgment turns out to be faster and cheaper—but only if you hire the right people and reward them for having the right attitude. Which is the attitude of a linchpin.

The Boss's Lie

"What I want is someone who will do exactly what I tell them to."

"What I want is someone who works cheap."

"What I want is someone who shows up on time and doesn't give me a hard time."

So, if this is what the boss really wants, how come the stars in the company don't follow these three rules? How come the people who get promoted and get privileges and expense accounts and are then wooed away to join other companies and get written up in the paper and have servants and coffee boys . . . how come those guys aren't the ones who do this stuff?

What the boss really wants is an artist, someone who changes every-thing, someone who makes dreams come true. What the boss really wants is someone who can see the reality of today and describe a better tomorrow. What the boss really wants is a linchpin.

If he can't have that, he'll settle for a cheap drone.

INDOCTRINATION: HOW WE GOT HERE

Mediocre Obedience

We've been taught to be a replaceable cog in a giant machine.
We've been taught to consume as a shortcut to happiness.
We've been taught not to care about our job or our customers.
And we've been taught to fit in.

None of these things helps you get what you deserve.

We've bought into a model that taught us to embrace the system, to spend for pleasure, and to separate ourselves from our work. We've been taught that this approach works, but it doesn't (not anymore). And this disconnect keeps us from succeeding, cripples the growth of our society, and makes us really stressed.

It seems "natural" to live the life so many of us live, but in fact, it's quite recent and totally manmade. We exist in a corporate manufacturing mindset, one so complete that anyone off the grid seems like an oddity. In the last few years, though, it's becoming clear that people who reject the worst of the current system are actually *more* likely to succeed.

Evolutionary biologist Stephen Jay Gould wrote, "Violence, sexism, and general nastiness are biological since they represent one subset of a possible range of behaviors. But peacefulness, equality and kindness are just as biological—and we may see their influence increase if we can create social structures that permit them to flourish."

To his thoughts I'd add that mediocre obedience is certainly something we're capable of, but if we take initiative and add a little bravery, artistic leadership is something that's equally (or more) possible and productive. We've been trained to believe that mediocre obedience is a genetic fact for most of the population, but it's interesting to note that this trait doesn't show up until *after* a few years of schooling.

Description of the Factory

"Factory" is a loaded term. It brings to mind car assembly lines or sweatshops. I'm talking about something much broader than that.

The Prudential Insurance offices in Newark are a factory, and so is the Department of Motor Vehicles office near your house. Each McDonald's franchise is quite deliberately set up as a factory, and so is the Goodwill distribution center that processes clothes to be sent overseas to raise money for a good cause.

I define a factory as an organization that has figured it out, a place where people go to do what they're told and earn a paycheck. Factories have been the backbone of our economy for more than a century, and without them we wouldn't have the prosperity we have today.

That doesn't mean you want to work in one.

You Get What You Focus On

Today, our leaders worry about things like global warming, security, limited resources, and maintaining our infrastructure. And boomers worry about getting old and finding a doctor they can afford.

A hundred years ago, our leaders worried about two things that seem truly archaic to us now:

How to find enough factory workers; and

How to avoid overproduction.

FACTORY WORKERS

Factories convert natural resources into salable products. They turn iron ore into steel and corn into Twinkies. A surplus of natural resources cuts your costs and increases your productivity.

If human beings are a natural resource for factories, then your goal as a factory owner is to get good ones, cheap. So captains of industry and government reorganized our society around this goal.

Does this sound like a conspiracy theory? Where do you think engineering colleges and nursing schools come from? Why else would we spend so much time and money creating a nationwide system of schools and push so hard for a factory-like command and control system for managing and producing students?

Yes, we need facts and rigor and systems. Yes, we need people to learn certain skills. But this isn't enough. It's the preliminary first step.

The launch of universal (public and free) education was a profound change in the way our society works, and it was a deliberate attempt to transform our culture. And it worked. We trained millions of factory workers.

AVOIDING OVERPRODUCTION

A huge concern among capitalists at the turn of the last century was that as factories got better and better at making stuff, there wouldn't be enough people to buy what they made. The problem wasn't production; it was consumption. The typical household spent a tiny fraction of what we do on everything in our budget.

In the 1890s, the typical teenager owned only a few items of clothing, consumed virtually no media, and owned no cosmetics. Only the truly rich had rooms and rooms of belongings they rarely used.

One of the wonderful by-products of universal education was the network effect that supports consumer goods. Once one person in your class or your town had a car, others needed one. Once someone added more rooms or had a second or third pair of shoes, you needed them, too.

In the space of two generations, we created a consumer culture. There wasn't one; then there was. Keeping up with the Joneses is not a genetic predisposition. It's an invented need, and a recent one.

The sign in front of your local public school could say:

Maplemere Public School

WE TRAIN THE FACTORY WORKERS OF TOMORROW. OUR GRADUATES ARE VERY GOOD AT FOLLOWING INSTRUCTIONS. AND WE TEACH THE POWER OF CONSUMPTION AS AN AID FOR SOCIAL APPROVAL.

It's almost impossible to imagine a school with a sign that said:

"We teach people to take initiative and become remarkable artists, to question the status quo, and to interact with transparency. And our graduates understand that consumption is not the answer to social problems."

And yet that might be exactly what we need.

From Superhero to Mediocreman (and Back Again)

Kids can do anything (except fly, which they really truly want to do).

Very few of us set out to be average or to be typical.

Then, somewhere along the way, the indoctrination kicks in and we start looking for a place to hide. We try to find a place where no one will discover how truly mediocre we actually are.

We want steady work, something that smooths out the bumps, a sinecure that will protect us.

If you're insecure, the obvious response to my call to become a linchpin is, "I'm not good enough at anything to be indispensable." The typical indoctrinated response is that great work and great art and remarkable output are the domain of *someone else*. You think that your job is to do the work that needs doing, anonymously.

Of course, this isn't true, but it's what you've been taught to believe.

I've been lucky enough to meet or work with thousands of remarkable linchpins. It appears to me that the only way they differ from a mediocre rule-follower is that they never bought into this self-limiting line of thought. That's it.

Perhaps they had a great teacher who lit a lamp for them. Perhaps a parent or a friend pushed them to refuse to settle. Regardless, the distinction between cogs and linchpins is largely one of attitude, not learning.

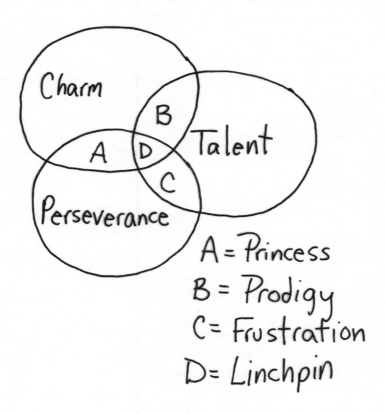

The Tiny Range of Motion

I watched author and conductor Roger Nierenberg teach a session using a symphony orchestra as an example. First, he asked the group to play the piece as well synchronized as possible. Then he had them do it again, asking each person to go to their own personal edge, engaging the music the way they wanted instead of the way the group wanted.

To the untrained ears in the room, the two versions were difficult to tell apart.

That's because we teach people to stick within a tiny range. We don't want the lows to be too low, so we limit the highs as well. The people in this orchestra couldn't even visualize themselves racing outside the box that had been established for them. Creativity is not choosing to wear a pink shirt to an office where only blue and white are standard. That's merely window dressing.

We see this in organizations of all types. We ask someone to do something wacky or original and they change the tiniest surface element instead of finding the root of a creative solution. That's no accident. That's what we taught them to do. The opportunity is in changing the game, changing the interaction, or even changing the question.

Fear at School

Studies show us that things learned in frightening circumstances are sticky. We remember what we learn on the battlefield, or when we burn a finger on a hot tea kettle. We remember what we learn in situations where successful action avoids a threat.

Schools have figured this out. They need shortcuts in order to successfully process millions of students a year, and they've discovered that fear is a great shortcut on the way to teaching compliance. Classrooms become fear-based, test-based battlefields, when they could so easily be organized to encourage the heretical thought we so badly need.

So, is it any surprise that people have learned to fit in, do the standardized test, keep heads down, obey instructions? Decades of school have drilled that into us—fear, fear, and more fear. Fear of getting a D-minus. Fear of not getting a job right out of school. Fear of not fitting in.

Well-intentioned teachers don't want to do this, but the system often gives them no choice. The work of creating positive change in a classroom is daunting, and without enough time and support, it's a tough slog.

Teaching people to produce innovative work, off-the-chart insights, and yes, art is time-consuming and unpredictable. Drill and practice and fear, on the other hand, are powerful tools for teaching facts and figures and obedience. Sure, we need school and we need teachers. The thing is that we need a school organized around teaching people to believe, and teachers who are rewarded for doing their *best* work, not the most predictable work.

Does School Work?

If I drill and practice and grade and reward you for years on doing math with fractions, what are the chances that you'll learn fractions? School does a great job of teaching students to do what we set out to teach them. It works. The problem is that what we're teaching is the wrong stuff.

Here's what we're teaching kids to do (with various levels of success):

Fit in

Follow instructions

Use #2 pencils

Take good notes

Show up every day

Cram for tests and don't miss deadlines

Have good handwriting

Punctuate

Buy the things the other kids are buying

Don't ask questions

Don't challenge authority

Do the minimum amount required so you'll have time to work on another subject

Get into college

Have a good résumé

Don't fail

Don't say anything that might embarrass you

Be passably good at sports, or perhaps extremely good at being a quarterback

Participate in a large number of extracurricular activities

Be a generalist

Try not to have the other kids talk about you

Once you learn a topic, move on

Now, the key questions:

Which of these attributes are the keys to being indispensable?

Are we building the sort of people our society needs?

The problem doesn't lie with the great teachers. Great teachers strive to create linchpins. The problem lies with the system that punishes artists and rewards bureaucrats instead.

Here's what Woodrow Wilson said about public education:

"We want one class of persons to have a liberal education, and we want another class of persons, a very much larger class, of necessity, in every society, to forgo the privileges of a liberal education and fit themselves to perform specific difficult manual tasks."

After retaining brutal Pinkerton men, trainloads of strikebreakers, and even the National Guard to violently put down strikes, Andrew Carnegie decided that the answer to worker unrest was a limited amount of education. "Just see, wherever we peer into the first tiny springs of the national life, how this true panacea for all the ills of the body politic bubbles forth—education, education, education."

The model is simple. Capitalists need compliant workers, workers who will be productive and willing to work for less than the value that their productivity creates. The gap between what they are paid and what the capitalist receives is profit.

The best way to increase profit was to increase both the productivity and the compliance of factory workers. And as Carnegie saw, the best way to do that was to build a huge educational-industrial complex designed to teach workers just enough to get them to cooperate.

It's not an accident that school is like a job, not an accident that there are supervisors and rules and tests and quality control. You do well, you get another job (the next grade), and continue to do well and you get a real job. Do poorly, don't fit in, rebel—and you are kicked out of the system.

"I Am Good at School"

This is a fundamentally different statement from, "I did well in school and therefore I will do a great job working for you." The essential thing measured by school is whether or not you are good at school.

Being good at school is a fine skill if you intend to do school forever. For the rest of us, being good at school is a little like being good at Frisbee. It's nice, but it's not relevant unless your career involves homework assignments, looking through textbooks for answers that are already known to your supervisors, complying with instructions and then, in high-pressure settings, regurgitating those facts with limited processing on your part. Or, in the latter case, if your job involves throwing 165 grams of round plastic as far as you can.

The contributions of school are often superfluous. On the other hand, the best schools are great selectors of people with attitude and talent. Getting in and getting out is a testament to who you were *before* you got there. Many successful people got that way despite their advanced schooling, not because of it.

What They Should Teach in School

Only *two things:*

1. Solve interesting problems
2. Lead

SOLVE INTERESTING PROBLEMS

"Interesting" is the key word. Answering questions like "When was the War of 1812?" is a useless skill in an always-on Wikipedia world. It's far more useful to be able to answer the kind of question for which using Google won't help. Questions like, "What should I do next?"

School expects that our best students will graduate to become trained trigonometricians. They'll be hired by people to compute the length of the hypotenuse of a certain right triangle. What a waste. The only reason to learn trigonometry is because it is a momentarily interesting question, one worth sorting out. But then we should move on, relentlessly seeking out new problems, ones even more interesting than that one. The idea of doing it by rote, of relentlessly driving the method home, is a total waste of time.

LEAD

Leading is a skill, not a gift. You're not born with it, you learn how. And schools can teach leadership as easily as they figured out how to teach compliance. Schools can teach us to be socially smart, to be open to connection, to understand the elements that build a tribe. While schools provide outlets for natural-born leaders, they don't teach it. And leadership is now worth far more than compliance is.

In Search of Great Teachers

Great teachers are precious. Lousy teachers cause damage that lasts forever.

We need to reorganize our schools to free the great teachers from tests and reports and busywork, and to expel the lousy teachers. I know this sounds like a pipe dream, but why should it be? When schools were organized to produce laborers, lousy teachers were exactly what we needed. Now, lousy teachers are dangerous.

Don't blame the teachers. Blame the corporate system that is still training compliant workers who test well.

BECOMING THE LINCHPIN

You Can't Get Far Without One

A linchpin is an unassuming piece of hardware, something you can buy for sixty-nine cents at the local hardware store. It's not glamorous, but it's essential. It holds the wheel onto the wagon, the thinger onto the widget.

Every successful organization has at least one linchpin; some have dozens or even thousands. The linchpin is the essential element, the person who holds part of the operation together. Without the linchpin, the thing falls apart.

Is there anyone in an organization who is absolutely irreplaceable? Probably not. But the most essential people are so difficult to replace, so risky to lose, and so valuable that they might as well be irreplaceable. Entire corporations are built around a linchpin, or more likely, a scattering of them, essential individuals who are worth holding on to.

1. Your business needs more linchpins. It's scary to rely on a particular employee, but in a postindustrial economy, you have no choice.

2. You are capable of becoming a linchpin. And if you do, you'll discover that it's worth the effort.

The easiest linchpin examples to find are CEOs and entrepreneurs, because they're the ones who get all the press. Steve Jobs at Apple or Jeff

Bezos at Amazon or Ben Zander at the Boston Philharmonic or Anne Jackson at flowerdust.net. We look at these leaders and say, "Of course they're the linchpin. That organization wouldn't be the same without them."

But what about that great guy down at the vegetable stand? You know, the one who makes it worth a special trip past the (cheaper and more convenient) supermarket. If he left, the place would go downhill and you'd stop going. All the rent, all the inventory, all the investment—they're worthless if he leaves. As far as you, the customer, are concerned, he's indispensable.

Have you ever purchased a car or consulting services or a house because the person you worked with made a powerful connection with you? If so, then she was the linchpin in the entire process. If she had been replaced by a cheaper, by-the-book automaton, you'd have bought from someone else. Indispensable.

What about the way it makes you feel when you walk into an Anthropologie store, or unwrap a piece of Lake Champlain chocolate, or send a package using FedEx's Web site? The experience could have been merely ordinary, merely another bit of good-enough. But it's not. It's magical. It was created by someone who cared, who contributed, who did more than he was told. A linchpin.

Anthropologie has a buyer, Keith Johnson, who spends six months a year traveling the world, visiting flea markets and garage sales, looking for extraordinary things. Not to sell, perhaps, but to beautify a store. It's not easy to hire a Keith Johnson, which is precisely why his work is so essential to their success.

If your organization would get out of the way, and if you would step up, there'd be a slot like that available. For anyone.

Creating Forward Motion

Imagine an organization with an employee who can accurately see the truth, understand the situation, and understand the potential outcomes of various decisions. And now imagine that this person is also able to make something happen.

Why on earth would you ever begin to consider the possibility of firing her? Inconceivable.

Every organization, every nonprofit, every political body, every corporation desperately seeks this person. This is our leader, our marketer, our linchpin. She creates forward motion.

There are bosses who might be threatened by someone who can create forward motion, but the shareholders and owners and board of every organization on earth desperately want forward motion. The distinction is subtle; calming your boss's anxiety is a first step in getting the organization to embrace the change you'll be making.

Doesn't matter if you're always right. It matters that you're always moving.

Linchpins and Leverage

You could do Richard Branson's job.

Most of the time, anyway.

I spent some time with Sir Richard, and I can tell you that you could certainly do most of what he does, perhaps better than he does it. Except for what he does for about five minutes a day. In those five minutes, he creates billions of dollars' worth of value every few years, and neither you nor I would have a prayer of doing what he does. Branson's real job is seeing new opportunities, making decisions that work, and understanding the connection between his audience, his brand, and his ventures.

The law of linchpin leverage: The more value you create in your job, the fewer clock minutes of labor you actually spend creating that value. In other words, most of the time, you're not being brilliant. Most of the time, you do stuff that ordinary people could do.

A brilliant author or businesswoman or senator or software engineer is brilliant only in tiny bursts. The rest of the time, they're doing work that most any trained person could do.

It might take a lot of tinkering or low-level work or domain knowledge for that brilliance to be evoked, but from the outside, it appears that the art is created in a moment, not in tiny increments.

This is more difficult if you have a job where your employer doesn't

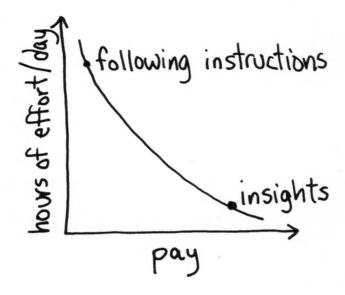

expect you to create much value. In these jobs, it's grunt work, hard work, and persistent work that creates value. Moving a pile of bricks from one place to another is important, but there is no expectation that you'll contribute bursts of brilliance. The boss believes that it is merely a slog.

Bricks need to be moved, of course. Understand that you don't have to be the one moving them as long as there's someone cheaper and more replaceable you can hire to do the moving. And if you've got no choice but to move the bricks, your opportunity is to think hard about how you do even this mundane task, because almost any job can be humanized or transformed.

It's difficult to train people to be Mark Cuban or Richard Branson or Madeleine Albright. It's easy to train people to do the slog stuff because there's a clear process and a manual. It's work. Any single person might not want to do it, but finding people who will do it isn't really a problem.

Inventing Twitter or Digg or 1-800-GOT-JUNK or Flatiron Partners, though, that takes something else. In 1996, Fred Wilson and Jerry Colonna founded a venture capital firm in New York City. Flatiron was the largest and most important Internet investment firm in New York, and for five years, they returned profits and created companies like few other funds in history. After the fact, it seems obvious that this was a special moment in time, and that taking advantage of it was smart. But right there, right then, it wasn't obvious, it wasn't easy, and there certainly wasn't a manual. Anyone could have done it, but anyone didn't. They did.

It takes art. Our economy now rewards artists far more than any other economy in history ever has.

People who tell you that they don't have any good ideas are selling themselves short. They don't have ideas that are valued because they're not investing in their art.

People who tell you that "I could paint a painting like that" are missing the point. The craft of the painting, the craft of writing that e-mail, the craft of building that PowerPoint presentation—those are the easy parts. It's the art and the insight and the bravery of value creation that are rewarded.

Massive Shift in the Leverage of Productivity

In a rigid, mechanized system (a factory!), the difference between a pretty good employee and a great employee is small.

A punch press operator might have a range of twenty to twenty-four units made in an hour. The best punch press operator in the world delivers about 20 percent more output than a pretty good punch press operator does.

On the other hand, the freestyle world of idea creation and idea manipulation offers dramatic differences between the merely good and the truly great. A great designer like Jonathan Ive is worth a hundred times as much as a good one. Where does Apple add value? If all MP3 players play the same music, why is an iPod worth so much more than a generic one? It's the breakthrough design that Ive pushed through at Apple. In fact, if you consider the relative stock prices and profits of Apple versus companies that hire standard designers to do ordinary work, there's really no comparison.

A great salesperson might deliver a thousand times as much productivity as a mediocre one. It's the great salesperson who opens an entire region or an account in a new industry, while the ordinary one merely goes down the call list, doing quite average work.

This is an astonishing piece of news. A very good senior programmer (who might get paid $200,000) gets paid about the same as a great programmer, who delivers $5 million worth of value for the same price. That's enough of a difference to build an entire company's profit around. Do it with ten programmers and you're rich.

Organizing around the average, then, is too expensive. Organizing around average means that the organization has exchanged the high productivity of exceptional performance for the ease and security of an endless parade of average performers.

The Tedium, Pain, and Insecurity of Being Mediocre

Not only do organizations benefit from linchpin employees, but employees also benefit once they become linchpins.

Finding security in mediocrity is an exhausting process. You can work only so many hours, fret only so much. Being a slightly better typist or a slightly faster coder is insufficient. You're always looking over your shoulder, always trying to be a little less mediocre than the guy next to you. It wears you out.

It's impossible to do the work at the same time you're in pain. The moment-to-moment insecurity of so many jobs robs you of the confidence you need to actually do great work.

On top of this, if you do great work you gain the reward of knowing you're doing great work. Your day snaps into alignment with your dreams, and you no longer have to pretend you're mediocre. You're free to contribute.

Does Every Organization Need Linchpins?

Do I want airline pilots and air traffic controllers making up new policies on the fly?

Do we want the hamburger flippers at McDonald's demanding more pay because their unique talents make them indispensable?

Should every interaction with the IRS be a freestyle improvisation?

Probably not.

Organizations that are centralized, monopolistic, static, safe, cost-sensitive, and far-flung should hire drones, as cheaply as possible.

Commodity producers in highly competitive businesses should do the same. If you're producing tires for Hyundai or light-bulb filaments for Sylvania, most of the people in your company need to be inexpensive first, reliable second, and present, third.

Hire cheap drones that you can scale, replace, and disrespect.

I have no issue at all with this as a business strategy. But I don't expect that it will lead to growth or significant customer loyalty, particularly in times of change.

More important, if you're looking for a job, I have no idea why you'd want to work in a company like this. Let someone else have that job. You deserve better.

Depth of Knowledge Alone Is Not Enough

Wikipedia and the shared knowledge of the Internet make domain knowledge on its own worth significantly less than it used to be. Today, if all you have to offer is that you know a lot of reference book information, you lose, because the Internet knows more than you do.

Depth of knowledge combined with good judgment is worth a lot. Depth of knowledge combined with diagnostic skills or nuanced insight is worth a lot, too. Knowledge alone, though, I'd rather get faster and cheaper from an expert I find online. If I need a great direct mail letter, it's far cheaper and faster to hire a great direct mail writer to write me a letter than it is to hire someone and have him on staff for the one letter I need every month, right?

Depth of knowledge is rarely sufficient, all by itself, to turn someone into a linchpin.

There are three situations where an organization will reward and embrace someone with extraordinary depth of knowledge:

1. When the knowledge is needed on a moment's notice and bringing in an outside source is too risky or time consuming.

2. When the knowledge is needed on a constant basis and the cost of bringing in an outside source is too high.

3. When depth of knowledge is also involved in decision making, and internal credibility and organizational knowledge go hand in hand with knowing the right answer.

It's easy for an outside source to be seen, in artist Julian Schnabel's words, as a "tourist." A tourist may have significant technical skill, but if she doesn't know the territory—your territory—then the skill isn't worthwhile.

On the other hand, as we have seen in the divergent paths of Rick Wagoner, the insider with domain knowledge who bankrupted General Motors, and Alan Mulally, the outsider with only clear vision, leadership skills, and a good posture who saved Ford, depth of knowledge alone is enough to get you into serious trouble.

A few years before Detroit's meltdown, Bill Ford knew his company was in jeopardy, so he went outside to hire a new CEO.

His biggest concern? "Ford is a place where they wait for the leader to tell them what to do."

Perhaps the biggest shift Alan Mulally made when he arrived from Boeing was changing that. Instead of hiring someone with deep domain knowledge who knew exactly what to do, Bill Ford hired someone who knew how to train people to live without a map.

Rick Wagoner lost his job at GM because he told everyone what to do (and he was wrong). Far better to build a team that figures out what to do instead.

The Best Reason to Be an Expert in Your Field

Expertise gives you enough insight to reinvent what everyone else assumes is the truth.

Sure, it's possible to randomly challenge the conventions of your field and luckily find a breakthrough. It's far more likely, though, that you will design a great Web site or direct a powerful movie or lead a breakthrough product development if you understand the status quo better than anyone else.

Beginner's luck is dramatically overrated.

Emotional Labor and Making Maps

"Emotional labor" was a term first coined forty years ago by sociologist Arlie Hochschild in her book *The Managed Heart*. She described it as the "management of feeling to create a publicly observable facial and bodily display." In other words, it's work you do with your feelings, not your body.

Emotional labor is the hard work of making art, producing generosity, and exposing creativity. Working without a map involves both vision and the willingness to do something about what you see.

Emotional labor is what you get paid to do, and one of the most difficult types of emotional labor is staring into the abyss of choice and picking a path.

Your Job Is a Platform

You get paid to go to work and do something of value. But your job is also a platform for generosity, for expression, for art.

Every interaction you have with a coworker or customer is an opportunity to practice the art of interaction. Every product you make represents an opportunity to design something that has never been designed, to create an interaction unlike any other.

For a long time, few people were fired for refusing to understand that previous paragraph. Now, though, it's not an option. It's the only reason you got paid to go to work today.

Degrees of Freedom

This is important.

One of the easy things about riding the train is that there aren't many choices. The track goes where the track goes. Sure, sometimes there are junctions and various routes, but generally speaking, there are only two choices—go or don't go.

Driving is a little more complicated. In a car you can choose from literally millions of destinations.

Organizations are far more complex. There are essentially an infinite number of choices, endless degrees of freedom. Your marketing can be free or expensive, online or offline, funny or sad. It can be truthful, emotional, boring, or bland. In fact, every marketing campaign ever done has been at least a little different from every other one.

The same choices exist in even greater number when you look at the microdecisions that go on every day. Should you go to a meeting or not? Shake hands with each person or just start? Order in fancy food for your guests or go for a walk together because the weather is sunny. . . .

In the face of an infinite sea of choices, it's natural to put blinders on, to ask for a map, to beg for instructions, or failing that, to do exactly what you did last time, even if it didn't work.

Linchpins are able to embrace the lack of structure and find a new path, one that works.

Marissa Mayer

What can she do that you can't?

Marissa has created billions of dollars' worth of value in her time at Google. Yet she's not the key brain in the programming department, nor is she responsible for finance or even public relations.

Marissa is a linchpin. She applies artistic judgment combined with emotional labor. She makes the interfaces work (the user interface and the interface between the engineers and the rest of the world) and leads the people who get things done.

Google works because the way the site takes your query and returns your results has such discipline and a clarity of vision that people prefer it even when the search results aren't any better than those provided by Yahoo or Microsoft. Google's now-cherished user interface is actually more valuable than their search technology. Marissa led the way in forcing Google's start page to be as spare as it is. She counts the number of words on that page and fights to keep the number as low as possible.

Google also works because the interface between the engineers and what the public wants and needs is so tight. Someone at Google has figured out how to help the company solve our problems (problems we didn't even know we had). Marissa is often in the position of being that interface.

She didn't get assigned either of those jobs. She just did them.

If you could write Marissa's duties into a manual, you wouldn't need her. But the minute you wrote it down, it wouldn't be accurate anyway. That's the key. She solves problems that people haven't predicted, sees things people haven't seen, and connects people who need to be connected.

Give Yourself a D

The A paper is banal.

Hand in a paper with perfect grammar but no heart or soul, and you're sure to get an A from the stereotypical teacher. That's because this teacher was trained to grade you on your ability to fit in. He's checking to see if you spelled "ubiquitous" properly and used it correctly. Whether or not your short story made him cry is irrelevant. And that's how school stamps out (as opposed to bakes in) insight and creativity.

My heroes Roz and Ben Zander wrote an incredible book called *The Art of Possibility*. One of the most powerful essays in the book describes how Ben changes the lives of his hyperstressed music students by challenging each of them to "give yourself an A." His point is that announcing in advance that you're going to do great—embracing your effort and visualizing an outcome—is far more productive than struggling to beat the curve.

I want to go farther than that.

I say you should give yourself a D (unless you're lucky enough to be in Ben's class). Assume before you start that you're going to create something that the teacher, the boss, or some other nitpicking critic is going to dislike. Of course, they need to dislike it for all the wrong reasons. You can't abandon technique merely because you're not good at it or unwilling to do the work. But if the reason you're going to get a D is that you're challenging structure and expectation and the status quo, then YES! Give yourself a D.

A well-earned D.

Who Are You Trying to Please?

If you seek out critics, bureaucrats, gatekeepers, form-fillers, and by-the-book bosses when you're looking for feedback, should you be surprised that you end up doing the things that please them?

They have the attitude that there is an endless line of cogs just like you, and you better fit in, bow down, and do what you're told, or they'll just go to the next person in line.

Without your consent, they can't hold on to the status quo, can't make you miserable, can't maintain their hold on power. It's up to you. You can spend your time on stage pleasing the heckler in the back, or you can devote it to the audience that came to hear you perform.

The Troubleshooter

Your restaurant has four waiters, and tough times require you to lay someone off.

Three of the waiters work hard. The other one is good, but is also a master at solving problems. He can placate an angry customer, finesse the balky computer system, and mollify the chef when he's had too much to drink.

Any idea who has the most secure job?

Troubleshooting is never part of a job description, because if you could describe the steps needed to shoot trouble, there wouldn't be trouble in the first place, right? Troubleshooting is an art, and it's a gift from the troubleshooter to the person in trouble. The troubleshooter steps in when everyone else has given up, puts himself on the line, and donates the energy and the risk to the cause.

Krulak's Law: Linchpins Whether You Want Them or Not

Jeff Sexton points out that ten years ago, General Charles Krulak theorized that in an age of always-on cameras, cell phones, and social networks, the lowly corporal in the field would have far more leverage and impact than ever before. He wrote, "In many cases, the individual Marine will be the most conspicuous symbol of American foreign policy and will potentially influence not only the immediate tactical situation, but the operational and strategic levels as well."

Krulak's law is simple: The closer you get to the front, the more power you have over the brand.

One errant minimum-wage cog in the machine can cripple an entire brand, or at the very least, wreck the lifetime value of a customer. The two kids at Domino's who made a YouTube sensation out of cruelty to pizza (and customers) did more damage to the Domino's brand than any vice president ever could.

If you think the solution is more rules and less humanity, I fear you will be disappointed by the results. Organizations that can bring humanity and flexibility to their interactions with other human beings will thrive.

Why We Started to Care

Of course, for decades, companies have been mechanizing production so that the opportunity for making a career out of following instructions and lifting heavy objects has gotten smaller and smaller. Of course, you didn't care so much, but the number of good jobs for manual laborers has been dropping for years. We've been eliminating machine operators and paint sprayers and other trades in order to lower costs.

The key is "we." The jobs being eliminated belonged to a class of people that was easy to ignore. We rationalized, because we were not being affected. It was efficient to eliminate blue-collar jobs; it made us competitive; it was progress.

Now, thanks to the information revolution and the law of the Mechanical Turk, the jobs that are disappearing belong to us, not those other people. Suddenly, we care a great deal about the jobs that have disappeared, probably forever. It bothers us because the jobs of people who followed the same rules we did are now in jeopardy.

A League of Your Own

Donald Bradman was an Australian cricket player. He was also the best athlete who ever lived. By any statistical measure, he was comparatively the best at what he did. He was far better at cricket than Michael Jordan was at basketball or Jack Nicklaus was at golf.

It's very difficult to be as good as Donald Bradman. In fact, it's impossible. Here's a chart of Bradman's batting average compared with the other all-time cricket leaders:

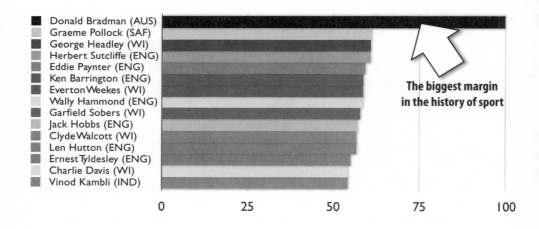

Everyone else is grouped quite near sixty. Bradman was in a league of his own, not even close to the others.

The challenge of becoming a linchpin solely based on your skill at plying a craft or doing a task or playing a sport is that the market can find other people with that skill with surprising ease. Plenty of people can play the flute as well as you can, clean a house as well as you can, program in Python as well as you can. If all you can do is the task and you're not in a league of your own at doing the task, you're not indispensable.

Statistics are a dangerous deal, because statistics make it strikingly clear that you're only a little better than the other guy. Or perhaps not better at all.

When you start down the path of beating the competition based on something that can be easily measured, you're betting that with practice and determination, you can do better than Len Hutton or Jack Hobbs did at cricket. Not a little better, but Don Bradman better.

And you can't.

On the Other Hand . . .

Being as charming as Julia Roberts or as direct as Marlon Brando or as provocative as Danny Boyle—that's way easier than playing cricket better than anyone who ever lived.

Emotional labor is available to all of us, but is rarely exploited as a competitive advantage. We spend our time and energy trying to perfect our craft, but we don't focus on the skills and interactions that will allow us to stand out and become indispensable to our organization.

Emotional labor was originally seen as a bad thing, a drain on the psyche of the stewardesses studied by Hochschild for her book. The mistake in her analysis was failing to consider the alternative. The alternative is working in a coal mine. The alternative is working in a sweatshop. It's called work because it's difficult, and emotional labor is the work most of us are best suited to do. It may be exhausting, but it's valuable.

(Colbert's Rapport)

Why do so many handmade luxury goods come from France?

It's not an accident. It's the work of one man, Jean-Baptiste Colbert. He served under Louis XIV of France in the 1600s and devised a plan to counter the imperialist success of the countries surrounding France. England, Portugal, Spain, and other countries were colonizing the world, and France was being left behind.

So Colbert organized, regulated, and promoted the luxury-goods industry. He understood what wealthy consumers around the world wanted, and he helped French companies deliver it. Let other countries find the raw materials; the French would fashion it, brand it, and sell it back to them as high-priced goods.

A critical element of this approach was the work of indispensable artisans. Louis Vuitton made his trunks by hand in a small workshop behind his house outside of Paris. Hermes would assign a craftsperson to work on a saddle for as long as it might take. The famous vintners of Champagne relied on trained professionals—men who had worked their whole lives with wine—to create a beverage that could travel around the world.

At the same time that France was embracing handmade luxury, Great Britain was embracing the anonymous factory. Looms that could turn out cotton cloth with minimal human labor, or pottery factories that could make cheap plates.

"Made in France" came to mean something (and still does, more than three hundred years later) because of the "made" part. Mechanizing and cheapening the process would have made it easy for others to copy. Relying on humanity made it difficult—it made the work done in France scarce, and scarcity creates value.

Fearless, Reckless, and Feckless

Organizations seek out people who are fearless, but go out of their way to weed out the reckless. What's the difference?

Fearless doesn't really mean "without fear." What it means in practice is, "unafraid of things that one shouldn't be afraid of." Being fearless means giving a presentation to an important customer without losing a night's sleep. It means being willing to take intellectual risks and to forge a new path. The fear is about an imagined threat, so avoiding the fear allows you to actually accomplish something.

Reckless, on the other hand, means rushing into places that only a fool would go. Reckless leads to huge problems, usually on the boss's dime. Reckless is what led us to the mortgage and liquidity crisis. Reckless is way out of style.

Feckless? Feckless is the worst of all. Ineffective, indifferent, and lazy.

Where Do You Put the Fear?

When men were building the railroads or when Mary Decker was setting records in the mile or ten thousand meters, it was clear that the key to success was dealing with fatigue. When you got tired, you didn't quit. If you quit, you lost (your job or the race). No one honestly asked, "Where do you put the tired?" but it's a fine question. Where did it go? The fatigue was there, but some people understood that putting it aside was the single most important factor in succeeding.

If you seek to become indispensable, a similar question is worth asking: "Where do you put the fear?" What separates a linchpin from an ordinary person is the answer to this question. Most of us feel the fear and react to it. We stop doing what is making us afraid. Then the fear goes away.

The linchpin feels the fear, acknowledges it, then proceeds. I can't tell you how to do this; I think the answer is different for everyone. What I can tell you is that in today's economy, doing it is a prerequisite for success.

The Problem with (Almost) Perfect

Asymptotes are sort of boring. An asymptote is a line that gets closer and closer and closer to perfection, but never quite touches.

If you make widgets and one out of ten is defective, improving quality has a huge amount of value, to you and to your customers.

Now, if one in a hundred is defective, an increase in quality is welcome, but not overwhelming.

Once you get to one defect in a thousand, that's pretty sweet, but certainly not perfect.

An increase to one in ten thousand as a defect rate is good enough for most things, except perhaps pacemakers.

An increase in quality to one in a hundred thousand is incredibly difficult to achieve, and it will get you a small raise.

An increase to one in a million, though, is so close to perfect that it's unlikely you'll even make a million units, so it's unnoticeable by anyone.

The chart of the asymptote looks like this:

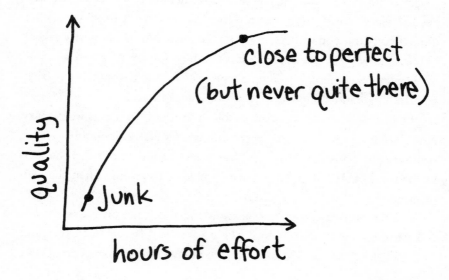

As you get closer to perfect, it gets more and more difficult to improve, and the market values the improvements a little bit less. Increasing your free-throw percentage from 98 to 99 percent may rank you better in the record books, but it won't win any more games and the last 1 percent takes almost as long to achieve as the first 98 percent did.

Ten percent of the applications to Harvard are from people who got a perfect score on their SATs. Approximately the same number are from people who were ranked first in their class. Of course, it's impossible to rank higher than first and impossible to get an 820, and yet more than a thousand in each group are rejected by Harvard every year. Perfection, apparently, is not sufficient.

Personal interactions don't have asymptotes. Innovative solutions to new problems don't get old. Seek out achievements where there is no limit.

Showstopper!

Two hours into *Guys and Dolls*, time stops.

Nathan Detroit walks out in his yellow overcoat, shouts out to Nicely Nicely Johnson, and then Johnson and the cast start belting: "Sit down, sit down, sit down, sit down, sit down you're rocking the boat!"

Adrenaline flows. The crowd goes wild.

In that moment, art triumphs over everything. The play has been rolling along, and suddenly the songs, the lights, the dancing—they're all taken up a notch (or ten). The crowd wakes up, leans forward, and cheers.

Consider the way a pilot walking down the aisle can change the entire afternoon for a restless kid on a flight. Or the way a doctor taking just an extra minute can change her relationship with a patient by pausing and caring.

The opposite of being a cog is being able to stop the show, at will. What would it take for you to stop the show?

The Pursuit of Perfect

How many of your coworkers spend all day in search of perfect?

Or, more accurately, spend all day trying to avoid making a mistake? These are very different things. Defect-free is what people are often in search of. Meeting spec. Blameless.

We've been trained since first grade to avoid mistakes. The goal of any test, after all, is to get 100 percent. No mistakes. Get nothing wrong and you get an A, right?

Read someone's résumé, and discover twenty years of extraordinary exploits and one typo. Which are you going to mention first?

We hire for perfect, we manage for perfect, we measure for perfect, and we reward for perfect.

So why are we surprised that people spend their precious minutes of self-directed, focused work time trying to achieve perfect?

The problem is simple: Art is never defect-free. Things that are remarkable never meet spec, because that would make them standard-ized, not worth talking about.

Rough Edges and Perfect

Bob Dylan knows a little about becoming indispensable, being an artist, and living on the edge:

> Daltrey, Townshend, McCartney, the Beach Boys, Elton, Billy Joel. They made perfect records, so they have to play them perfectly . . . exactly the way people remember them. My records were never per-fect. So there is no point in trying to duplicate them. Anyway, I'm no mainstream artist.
>
> . . . I guess most of my influences could be thought of as eccen-tric. Mass media had no overwhelming reach so I was drawn to the traveling performers passing through. The side show performers—bluegrass singers, the black cowboy with chaps and a lariat doing rope tricks. Miss Europe, Quasimodo, the Bearded Lady, the half-man half-woman, the deformed and the bent, Atlas the Dwarf, the fire-eaters, the teachers and preachers, the blues singers. I remem-ber it like it was yesterday. I got close to some of these people. I learned about dignity from them. Freedom too. Civil rights, human rights. How to stay within yourself. Most others were into the rides like the tilt-a-whirl and the roller-coaster. To me that was the night-mare. All the giddiness. The artificiality of it . . .

The interviewer then reminded Dylan, "But you've sold over a hun-dred million records."

Dylan's answer gets to the heart of what it means to be an artist: "Yeah I know. It's a mystery to me too."

Avoiding the treadmill of defect-free is not easy to sell to someone who's been trained in the perfection worldview since first grade (which is most of us). But artists embrace the mystery of our genius instead. They understand that there is no map, no step-by-step plan, and no way to avoid blame now and then.

If it wasn't a mystery, it would be easy. If it were easy, it wouldn't be worth much.

The Problem with Bowling

Bowling is an asymptotic sport. The best you can do is perfect: 300, that's it. There's a ceiling.

This is like the Six Sigma approach to quality. Six Sigma refers to the quest for continuous improvement, ultimately leading to 3.4 defects per million units. The problem is that once you're heading down this road, there's no room left for amazing improvements and remarkable innovations. Either you rolled ten strikes or you didn't.

Organizations that earn dramatic success always do it in markets where asymptotes don't exist, or where they can be shattered. If you could figure out how to bowl 320, that would be amazing. Until that happens, pick a different sport if you want to be a linchpin.

The Downside of Good

Being pretty good is extremely easy these days. Building a pretty good Web site, for example, is significantly cheaper and faster and easier than building a pretty good storefront was twenty years ago. Same goes for writing a pretty good e-mail message, one that can compare with something from a giant corporation, or shipping a package across the country.

The record you can cut in your basement or the food you can prepare with ingredients from the local market—all pretty good. You can buy a world-class CD player for twenty-nine dollars and hire a great lawyer by investing a few clicks and a phone call.

Employees are encouraged to deliver products and services and inputs that are good. Good as in within the boundaries defined by the boss. Showing up at the beginning of your shift and staying to the end is good. Meeting spec is good. Answering the phone in a reasonable amount of time is good.

The problem with meeting expectations is that it's not remarkable. It won't change the recipient of your work, and it's easy to emulate (which makes you easy to replace). As a result of the tsunami of pretty good (and the persistence of really lousy), the market for truly exceptional is better than ever. That's what I want if I hire someone for more than what the market will bear—someone exceptional.

So yes, good is bad, if bad means "not a profitable thing to aspire to." And perfect is bad, because you can't top perfect. The solution lies in seeking out something that is neither good nor perfect. You want something remarkable, nonlinear, game changing, and artistic.

Work is a chance to do art. Good art is useless and banal. No one crosses the street to buy good art, or becomes loyal to a good artist.

If you can't be remarkable, perhaps you should consider doing nothing until you can. If your organization skipped a month's catalog because you didn't have anything great to put in it, what would happen the next month? Would the quality and user delight of your product line improve?

Raising the bar is easier than it looks, and it pays for itself. If your boss won't raise your bar, you should.

He Works for Blessings

David has been working in the midtown branch of Dean & Deluca for six years. This mini-chain of high-end coffee shops in New York has very high turnover, so six years is quite an achievement.

I met David while having coffee with a friend. The first thing I noticed was that he had walked over to a line of tourists and cheerfully said, "Hey, guys! We have another bathroom upstairs. No need to wait." With a smile, he moved away, energetically cleaning off tables and straightening things that didn't seem particularly crooked to me. If this was menial labor, no one told David.

As the hour wore on, I saw him greet people, help without asking, offer to watch a table or get something for someone. In a coffee shop!

I asked him about his attitude. He smiled, stopped for a second, and told me, "I work for blessings."

Almost anyone else would have seen this job as a grind, a dead end, a mind-numbing way to spend six years. David saw it as an opportunity to give gifts. He had emotional labor to contribute, and his compensation was the blessings he got from the customers (his customers). His art was the engagement with each person, a chance to change her outlook or brighten his day. Not everyone can do this, and many who can, choose not to. David refused to wait for instructions. He led with his art.

The Work Whisperer

Monty Roberts is a horse whisperer. He listens to racehorses and then sets them free to be horses, to do what comes naturally, not what they were forced to do.

For generations, we've been pushing workers to do something inherently unnatural. We've been teaching, cajoling, and yes, forcing people to hide their empathy and their creativity and to pretend that they are fast-moving automatons, machines designed to do the company's bidding.

It's not necessary. No, I'll go further than that: it's damaging. It's damaging to have to put on a new face for work, the place we spend our days. It's damaging to build organizations around repetitive faceless work that brings no connection and no joy.

As our economy has matured and mechanized, seeking out and adhering to the norm has become unprofitable. It's unprofitable to establish a career around the idea of doing what the manual says.

So, consider this your whispered call to freedom. The world wants you (needs you) to bring your genius self to work.

Do You Need a Résumé?

This is controversial, but here goes: if you're remarkable, amazing, or just plain spectacular, you probably shouldn't have a résumé at all.

If you've got experience in doing the things that make you a linchpin, a résumé hides that fact.

A résumé gives the employer everything she needs to reject you.

Once you send me your résumé, I can say, "Oh, they're missing this or they're missing that," and boom, you're out.

Having a résumé begs for you to go into that big machine that looks for relevant keywords, and begs for you to get a job as a cog in a giant machine. More fodder for the corporate behemoth. That might be fine for average folks looking for an average job, but is that what you deserve?

The very system that produced standardized tests and the command-and-control model that chokes us also invented the résumé. The system, the industrialists, the factory . . . they want us to be cogs in their machine—easily replaceable, hopeless, cheap cogs.

If you don't have a résumé, what do you have?

How about three extraordinary letters of recommendation from people the employer knows or respects?

Or a sophisticated project an employer can see or touch?

Or a reputation that precedes you?

Or a blog that is so compelling and insightful that they have no choice but to follow up?

Some say, "Well, that's fine, but I don't have those."

Yeah, that's my point. If you don't have these things, what leads you to believe that you are remarkable, amazing, or just plain spectacular? It sounds to me like if you don't have more than a résumé, you've been brainwashed into compliance.

Great jobs, world-class jobs, jobs people kill for—those jobs don't get filled by people e-mailing in résumés.

Google You

Google "Jay Parkinson" and you will discover a doctor who is changing the U.S. health care system, virtually single-handedly.

Google "Sasha Dichter" and you will discover a visionary who is remaking philanthropy for the developing world.

Google "Louis Monier" and you will find a search engine guru whom you might be desperate to hire for your next start-up.

There are tens of thousands of linchpins like these, people who have the work, not just a résumé. And the work is exactly what the linchpin's résumé looks like. Two of the three people listed above aren't entrepreneurs. They have jobs. That's a huge shift from just a few years ago, when the work you did inside of an organization was almost entirely anonymous. The Internet shines a light on your projects.

The only way to prove (as opposed to assert) that you are an indispensable linchpin—someone worth recruiting, moving to the top of the pile, and hiring—is to show, not tell. Projects are the new résumés.

If your Google search isn't what you want (need) it to be, then change it.

Change it through your actions and connections and generosity. Change it by so over-delivering that people post about you. Change it by creating a blog that is so insightful about your area of expertise that others refer to it. And change it by helping other people online.

The long tail that Chris Anderson wrote about doesn't apply only to CDs and books. It applies to people, too. Sure, there are "hits" like rock stars or politicians or CEOs. But there's also room for everyone who wants to make a difference. It doesn't matter where you live on the long tail, as long as the tribe of people you connect with are eager to seek you out and help you succeed.

How to Get a Great Job

A lot of this discussion begs the question: If you're a linchpin, indispensable, worth hiring, and able to make a difference, how do you get a job in a world filled with me-too résumés and factories?

If that is the question, you don't. You won't often be able to persuade the standardized HR system to make an exception. A better plan: find a company that understands the value of the linchpin. Find a company that doesn't use a computer to scan résumés, a company that hires people, not paper.

Jason Zimdars is a linchpin. He's a graphic designer living in Oklahoma and he has design chops that any smart company would kill for. It took Jason a year to get a job working for 37signals, a cutting-edge software company in Chicago. How did they find each other?

It wasn't his résumé. Over the course of the year, Jason corresponded with people at the company. He didn't send in a boring résumé, he talked to them about his work and their needs. They hired him to do a freelance project. He excelled at that, so they gave him an assignment on spec. You can see the page he built online: http://jasonzimdars.com/svn/highrise .html.

Two things were at work here. First, 37signals is a company dedicated to hiring only linchpins. They reject the traditional pump-and-dump approach to hiring, and they're not indulging their egos by hiring people dumber than they are. Second, Jason is really good at what he does and he's willing to stand up and be recognized for his work. You are not your résumé. You are your work.

If the game is designed for you to lose, don't play that game. Play a different one.

Hiring at IDEO

Blogger Andrew Chen reports design firm IDEO is hiring marketers using a new technique. They ask applicants to make a PowerPoint presentation of their résumé and then present it to a group of five or six people at the firm. The applicant has to defend the work, answer questions, and lead a discussion.

One more chance to stand out, not to fit in. One more way to discover who has the actual skills (engagement, rapport, intellect, charisma, openness) to thrive in a modern work environment.

Saying No

There are two ways the linchpin can use "no."

The first is to never use it. There's a certain sort of indispensable team member who always finds a yes. She always manages to find a way to make things happen, and she does it. It's done. Yes.

Those people are priceless.

Amazingly, there's a second kind of linchpin. This person says "no" all the time. She says no because she has goals, because she's a practical visionary, because she understands priorities. She says no because she has the strength to disappoint you now in order to delight you later.

When used with good intent, this negative linchpin is also priceless. She is so focused on her art that she knows that a no now is a worthy investment for the magic that will be delivered later.

How to Make the Olympic Ski Team

Matt Dayton skied Nordic (cross-country) in the 2002 Olympics. He taught me a simple lesson: The person who leans forward the most wins the race.

In *The Dip*, I wrote about the challenge of persevering through a problem that causes most people to quit. In a race, sooner or later there's a moment that separates the winner from those who don't win. That instant is your chance, the moment you've been waiting for.

Consider the airline business. Everyone has to use similar planes and similar airports. There's no standardized opportunity to do better or worse than anyone else. But when it comes to pricing or service or enthusiasm, you get a chance to play by different rules from the competition. And the brand that leans into the problem the hardest will win.

The linchpin brings the ability to lean.

He can find a new solution to a problem that has caused others to quit. His art, his genius, is to reimagine the opportunity and find a new way to lean into it.

You may say, "But I'll get fired for breaking the rules." The linchpin says, "If I lean enough, it's okay if I get fired, because I'll have demonstrated my value to the marketplace. If the rules are the only thing between me and becoming indispensable, I don't need the rules."

It's easy to find a way to spend your entire day doing busywork. Trivial work doesn't require leaning. The challenge is to replace those tasks with rule-breaking activities instead.

Posture for Change

If I tell you to stand by, you'll simply stand. You can stand by on a corner or at a desk or in a job. Standing by requires a certain posture, because you may be doing it for a while.

If, on the other hand, I ask you to move a couch, dislodge a stuck door, or otherwise cause change in your environment, you won't do it from the same posture. You'll choose to lean into the task, because if you don't transfer your weight, you have no chance of moving anything.

The linchpin understands that this choice of posture is the critical step. Consider the customer service troubleshooter, the dervish who walks into any situation and makes it better. Her posture is forward; she's looking for opportunities. She wants to mix it up. She looks for trouble; trouble gives her a chance to delight.

The cog is standing by, waiting for instructions.

I still remember two jobs where I was required to stand by. I hated each one. I melted. Once, it was only for three days, but spending three days with a posture that was alien to me was incredibly difficult.

If you are hiring for a standy job, it won't attract linchpins.

The physical (and mental) posture of someone creating art both changes and causes change.

If you can, visualize the reluctant student, head on his shoulder, slumped on the desk, chewing on a pencil. This is student as employee, student as prisoner. The chances of great work or great learning occurring are zero. And so there's no transfer of positive emotion, no energy going back to the teacher or being spread to fellow students.

The same posture afflicts fast-food workers, overworked attorneys, and everyone in between.

But imagine an artist in the same situation. He's barely restrained, chomping to get to work. He leans into the work, not away from it. His energy creates energy in those around him; his charisma turns into leadership.

Art changes posture and posture changes innocent bystanders.

Unsolicited Advice for Steve

Steve works at the Stop & Shop near my house. He hates it. He works the cash register, and it seems as though every ounce of his being projects his dissatisfaction with his job.

Steve won't make eye contact.

Steve takes a lot of breaks.

Steve doesn't start bagging until the last possible moment.

Steve grumbles a lot.

The thing is, Steve spends as much time at work as Melinda. And Melinda is engaged and connected and enthusiastic. Steve has decided that he's not being paid enough to bring his entire self to work, and he's teaching all of us a lesson. Melinda has decided that she has a platform, and she uses it to make a tiny difference in every customer's day.

The Stop & Shop has to accept part of the blame for Steve's situation. First, they don't do anything at all to reward people who are generous. I've never seen a manager there go out of his way to respect or acknowledge great behavior. Melinda is going to leave soon, and good for her.

The really telling clue about the situation? Near the exit is a terminal where entry-level workers can apply for a job without engaging with a human being. Type in your data and you're hired. It communicates really clearly: "You're a cog, you're replaceable, there's someone coming in right behind you. Hey, we don't even have to meet you!"

When you offer the job of last resort, often people respond in kind.

The sad part for me is that while Steve is busy teaching the store a lesson, he's teaching himself that this is the way to do his job. He's fully expecting that his next job, or the job after that or the job after that—that's when he'll become the linchpin. If he waits for a job to be good enough to deserve his best shot, it's unlikely that he'll ever have that job.

What's in It for Me

Author Richard Florida polled twenty thousand creative professionals and gave them a choice of thirty-eight factors that motivated them to do their best at work.

The top ten, ranked in order:

1. Challenge and responsibility
2. Flexibility
3. A stable work environment
4. Money
5. Professional development
6. Peer recognition
7. Stimulating colleagues and bosses
8. Exciting job content
9. Organizational culture
10. Location and community

Only one of these is a clearly extrinsic motivator (#4, money). The rest are either things we do for ourselves or things that we value because of who we are.

The interesting thing about money is that there's no easy way for an employee to make it increase, at least not in the short run. Most of the other elements, though, can go through the roof as a result of our behavior, contributions, attitude, and gifts.

And yet, cynical management acts like a factory, figuring that the only motivators are cash and freedom from scolding.

Remarkable People Deserve Remarkable Jobs

If the mantra of the last era was "average jobs for average people, and average people for average jobs," then it's no surprise that most of the jobs out there seemed average, and that if you wanted to maximize your chances of getting one, fitting in was your best strategy.

Often, when people hear about my radical ideas for how you should train for a career, as well as the best way to present yourself, they object. They point out that not fitting in is certainly going to be an ineffective way of getting one of these average jobs. They remind me that not having a résumé is all fine and good, but how will that help them get a job at a place that requires a résumé?

You can't win both games—not at the same time, anyway.

If you want a job where you are treated as indispensable, given massive amounts of responsibility and freedom, expected to expend emotional labor, and rewarded for being a human, not a cog in a machine, then please don't work hard to fit into the square-peg job you found on Craigslist.

If you need to conceal your true nature to get in the door, understand that you'll probably have to conceal your true nature to keep that job. This is the one and only decision you get to make. You get to choose. You can work for a company that wants indispensable people, or you can work for a company that works to avoid them.

Groucho Marx famously said, "I don't care to belong to any club that would have me as a member."

The linchpin says, "I don't want a job that a non-linchpin could get."

IS IT POSSIBLE TO DO
HARD WORK IN A CUBICLE?

Labor Means Difficult

Apparently, we don't have a lot of trouble understanding that work might involve physical labor, heavy lifting, or long periods of fatigue. But, for some reason, we hesitate to invest a more important sort of labor into work that really matters. Emotional labor is the task of doing important work, even when it isn't easy.

Emotional labor is difficult and easy to avoid. But when we avoid it, we don't do much worth seeking out. Showing up unwilling to do emotional labor is a short-term strategy now, because over time, organizations won't pay extra for someone who merely does the easy stuff.

We're not at all surprised when a craftsman sharpens his saw or an athlete trains hard. But when an information worker develops her skills at confronting fear (whether it's in making connections, speaking, inventing, selling, or dealing with difficult situations) we roll our eyes.

It turns out that digging into the difficult work of emotional labor is exactly what we're expected (and needed) to do. Work is nothing but a platform for art and the emotional labor that goes with it.

Volunteering to Do Emotional Labor

"Cellphonesandpagersmustremainoffduringtheentireflighttheflightattendantsaregoingtobegintheirinflight . . ." The flight attendant read the script as fast as she possibly could. She had read it a thousand times before and she was going to read it a thousand more times. And she knew that not one passenger was going to listen to her.

In her frustration, she followed the rules, but barely. She read the script. But she didn't do the emotional labor that would have made her hard to replace.

When her airline loses even more money, when they replace the script with an audio recording, when they break the union and refuse to pay high wages to employees who don't add any value—well, she'll be even more frustrated then.

The opportunity doesn't necessarily feel like an opportunity. Volunteering to do emotional labor—even when you don't feel like it, and especially when you're not paid extra for it—is a difficult choice. My first argument, though, is that you *are* paid for it. In fact, in most jobs that involve a customer, that's *all* you are getting paid for.

For years, people chose to fly on JetBlue for two reasons. First, it was reasonably priced. And second, the flight attendants were terrific. Along with the pilots, the young and motivated staff worked as hard as they could to make the flight more fun. Notice that I said "as hard as they could." No doubt it wasn't easy to put on this show six times a day; no doubt there were times the staff would have preferred to have a map, a manual, an instruction guide on how to be pleasant and personable and memorable. But Amy Curtis-McIntyre, who developed JetBlue's shtick, refused to give them one. (And if she had wanted to, it's unlikely she could have.) Instead, she hired friendly people and motivated them to perform emotional labor.

The result? An asset was built, a brand was born, profits were made, and the airline grew.

Now, JetBlue has to choose: should they cut corners and be difficult with the very flight attendants who are a key marketing element of their success? Or should they embrace the fact that one of the linchpins of the airline is a motivated and connected staff that rewards passengers for choosing the airline?

The Gift of Emotional Labor

"The gift is to the giver, and comes back to him . . ."

—Walt Whitman

When you do emotional labor, you benefit.

Not just the company, not just your boss, but you.

The act of giving someone a smile, of connecting to a human, of taking initiative, of being surprising, of being creative, of putting on a show—these are things that we do for free all our lives. And then we get to work and we expect to merely do what we're told and get paid for it.

This gulf creates tension. If you reserve your emotional labor for when you are off duty, but you work all the time, you are deprived of the joy you get when you do this labor. Now, you're not giving gifts on duty, but you're not off duty much at all. Spend eight or ten or twelve hours a day at work (not only in the office, but online or on the phone or in your dreams), and there's not a lot of time left for the very human acts that make you who you are and who you want to be.

So bring that gift to work.

And what do you get in return? As we saw in the case of JetBlue, there are companies that now value this sort of labor and encourage it. More organizations (regardless of the state of the economy, or possibly because of the state of the economy) are embracing this idea and hiring for it and rewarding it.

In most cases, though, you get little in return. At least, little in terms of formal entries in your permanent file or bonuses in your year-end pay. But you do benefit. First, you benefit from the making and the giving. The act of the gift is in itself a reward. And second, you benefit from the response of those around you. When you develop the habit of contributing this gift, your coworkers become more open, your boss becomes more flexible, and your customers become more loyal.

The essence of any gift, including the gift of emotional labor, is that you don't do it for a tangible, guaranteed reward. If you do, it's no longer a gift; it's a job. The hybrid economy we're living in today is blending the idea of capitalism ("do your job and I won't fire you") and the gift economy ("wow, this is amazing").

Artists Who Can't Draw

Roy Simmons coined that phrase and I like it a lot. "Most artists can't draw."

We need to add something: "But all artists can see."

We can see what's right and what's wrong. We can see opportunities and we can see around corners. Most of all, we can see art.

Art isn't only a painting. Art is anything that's creative, passionate, and personal. And great art resonates with the viewer, not only with the creator.

What makes someone an artist? I don't think it has anything to do with a paintbrush. There are painters who follow the numbers, or paint billboards, or work in a small village in China, painting reproductions. These folks, while swell people, aren't artists. On the other hand, Charlie Chaplin was an artist, beyond a doubt. So is Jonathan Ive, who designed the iPod. You can be an artist who works with oil paints or marble, sure. But there are artists who work with numbers, business models, and customer conversations. Art is about intent and communication, not substances.

An artist is someone who uses bravery, insight, creativity, and boldness to challenge the status quo. And an artist takes it personally.

That's why Bob Dylan is an artist, but an anonymous corporate hack who dreams up Pop 40 hits on the other side of the glass is merely a marketer. That's why Tony Hsieh, founder of Zappos, is an artist, while a boiler room of telemarketers is simply a scam.

Tom Peters, corporate gadfly and writer, is an artist, even though his readers are businesspeople. He's an artist because he takes a stand, he takes the work personally, and he doesn't care if someone disagrees. His art is part of him, and he feels compelled to share it with you because it's important, not because he expects you to pay him for it.

Art is a personal gift that changes the recipient. The medium doesn't matter. The intent does.

Art is a personal act of courage, something one human does that creates change in another.

The thing about the paintings called modern art is that seeing them leads to a lot of discussion about the nature of art. "I could do that" is something you hear a lot.

If Jackson Pollock is art and Andy Warhol is art and performance art is art . . . then what is art? It's not about the craft, certainly. If Shakespeare is art and Sam Shepard is art, and Eric Bogosian is art, then Jerry Seinfeld must be art, too, right?

Is it art when Harvard scientist Jill Bolte Taylor holds us spellbound for eighteen minutes talking about her near-fatal stroke? Certainly.

And I think it's art when a great customer service person uses a conversation to convert an angry person into a raving fan. And it's art when Craig Newmark invents a new business model that uses the Internet to revolutionize the classifieds. Or when Ed Sutt invents a better nail, one that saves lives and money.

The semantics matter here, because we're going to explore what it is to make art, and we need to decide what art is before we can determine if that's useful to you. So, back to my definition:

Art is a personal gift that changes the recipient.

An artist is an individual who creates art. The more people you change, the more you change them, the more effective your art is.

Art is not related to craft, except to the extent that the craft helps deliver the change. Technical skill might be a helpful component in making art, but it's certainly not required. Art doesn't have to be decorative; it can be useful as long as the use causes change.

Art is certainly not limited to painting or sculpture or songwriting. If there is no change, there is no art. If no one experiences it, there can be no change.

By definition, art is human. A machine can't create art, because the intent matters. It's much more likely to be art if you do it on purpose.

A cook is not an artist. A cook follows a recipe, and he's a good cook if he follows the recipe correctly. A chef is an artist. She's an artist when she invents a new way of cooking or a new type of dish that creates surprise or joy or pleasure for the person she created it for.

Art is original. Marcel Duchamp was an artist when he pioneered Dadaism and installed a urinal in a museum. The second person to install a urinal wasn't an artist, he was a plumber.

Art is the product of emotional labor. If it's easy and risk free, it's unlikely that it's art.

The last element that makes it art is that it's a gift. You cannot create a piece of art merely for money. Doing it as part of commerce so denudes art of wonder that it ceases to be art. There's always a gift intent on the part of the artist.

Organizations use human-created art all the time. The design of the iPhone is art. It changes the way some people feel. It changes the way they use the device. It changes the way they communicate. And there is a gift as well. People who see the iPhone but don't buy one still receive the gift. An ugly iPhone would cost as much as the beautiful one. The beautiful part is the free prize inside, the bonus, the gift to us from the artist who designed it.

The Art of Interaction

Most artists (in our imagination) interact with stones or canvas or oil or words on paper. They do this before their work hits the viewer, causing an interaction or change to happen.

But the most visceral art is direct. One to one, mano a mano, the artist and the viewer. It's the art of interaction. It's what you do.

The art of running a meeting, counseling a student, conducting an interview, and calming an angry customer. The art of raising capital, buying a carpet at a souk, or managing a designer.

If art is a human connection that causes someone to change his mind, then you are an artist.

What if you were great at it?

There's a Village in China

Outside of Shenzhen lies Dafen. It's said that 60 percent of all the paintings in the world are produced by painters who live in this town.

Notice I said "painters," not "artists." That's because the workers in Dafen, while diligent and talented, aren't artists. They are cogs in a painting machine.

I own two paintings from Dafen. They are beautifully executed large paintings of stupid monkeys in ill-fitting clothes. One is a male chimp with a beanie, a propeller, and earrings. The other is a baby orangutan with a bow in her hair.

I got them on eBay, shipped (framed) directly from Dafen, for sixty dollars each.

Who knows which Dafen resident painted them? No one. Who cares? No one. The painters are replaceable; they are human machines thrown against a large problem, producing little bits of value each day.

The real artists are the people who dreamed up this system, or possibly the person who drew the first example of my little chimp man. But not the painters. They're virtually helpless victims of a large system that pays them very little for the talent they bring to work each day.

Gifts and Art and Emotional Labor

Art is created by an artist.

Art is unique, new, and challenging to the status quo. It's not decoration, it's something that causes change.

Art cannot be merely commerce. It must also be a gift. The artist creates his idea knowing that it will spread freely, without recompense. Sure, the physical manifestation of the art might sell for a million dollars, but that painting or that song is also going to be enjoyed by someone who didn't pay for it.

Art is not limited to art school, or to music or even to the stage. Art is any original idea that can be a gift. It takes art to make a mom happy on the first day of nursery school. It takes art to construct a business model that permits people in the United States to play poker online. It takes art to construct the plans for the English Chunnel.

Most of all, art involves labor. Not the labor of lifting a brush or typing a sentence, but the emotional labor of doing something difficult, taking a risk and extending yourself.

It's entirely possible that you're an artist.

Sometimes, though, caught up in the endless cycle of commerce, we forget about the gift nature of art, we fail to do the hard work of emotional labor, and we cease to be artists.

Selling Yourself Short

A day's work for a day's pay (work <=> pay). I hate this approach to life. It cheapens us.

This simple formula bothers me for two reasons:

1. Are you really willing to sell yourself out so cheap? Do you mortgage an entire (irreplaceable) day of your life for a few bucks? The moment you are willing to sell your time for money is the moment you cease to be the artist you're capable of being.

2. Is that it? Is the transaction over? If we're even at the end of the day as the formula says, then you owe me nothing and I owe you nothing in return. If we're even, then there is no bond, no ongoing connection between us. It's like Hector in Queens. You have become a day laborer and I have become a day boss.

The alternative is to treasure what it means to do a day's work. It's our one and only chance to do something productive today, and it's certainly not available to someone merely because he is the high bidder. A day's work is your chance to do art, to create a gift, to do something that matters. As your work gets better and your art becomes more important, competition for your gifts will increase and you'll discover that you can be choosier about whom you give them to.

When a day's work does not equal a day's pay, that means that at the end of the day, a bond is built. A gift is given and received, and people are drawn closer, not insulated from each other.

Passion

Passion is a desire, insistence, and willingness to give a gift. The artist is relentless. She says, "I will not feel complete until I give a gift." This is more than refusing to do lousy work. It's an insistence on doing important work.

This relentless passion leads to persistence and resilience in the face of people not accepting your gift.

The artists in your life are gift-focused, and their tenacity has nothing at all to do with income or job security. Instead, it's about finding a way to change you in a positive way, and to do it with a gift. There's a strong streak of intellectual integrity involved in being a passionate artist. You don't sell out, because selling out involves destroying the best of what you are.

Consider the case of Ed Sutt. The son of a contractor, Ed grew up helping his dad build houses—he eventually gave it up when he discovered that his hand was so swollen from hammering nails while framing new houses that he couldn't even see his knuckles.

Doing research at Clemson University's Wind Load Test Facility, Sutt studied the science of building and the effect of wind on wood frame houses. Along the way, he visited the Caribbean and saw the effects of Hurricane Marilyn. Thousands of houses were destroyed by the hurricane, completely disintegrated by the wind. While it certainly changed the lives of the people on the island, it changed Ed's life just as much.

Until that moment, the conventional wisdom was simple: if you wanted to have a chance to survive a hurricane, you had to build a very expensive house using expensive materials. The only alternative was a disposable wood frame house, one that was cheap but not particularly durable.

Popular Science reports: "The destruction was so complete in places that it was almost surreal," Sutt recalls. "There were troops in the streets and military helicopters hovering overhead." As Sutt moved through the wreckage of roofless and toppled-over houses, he was struck by the sense that much of the destruction could have been avoided. "In house after house," he says, "I noticed that it wasn't the wood that had failed—it was the nails that held the wood together."

He devoted the next eleven years (day and night) to creating a nail that would change the fate of millions of people. Sutt had the insight that it was a nail, not the rest of the house, that mattered. But the insight without dogged persistence over a decade would have been worthless.

You could argue that the millions of dollars that Sutt has earned in return for his invention was money well earned, that it repaid him handsomely for his passion. There's no doubt in my mind, though, that he would have done it for free. The passion wasn't in making the money—it was in making a difference, solving a problem, creating a change that would help millions. Ed Sutt is an artist, someone who chose to make a difference instead of following a manual.

"Wait! Are You Saying That I Have to Stop Following Instructions and Start Being an Artist? Someone Who Dreams Up New Ideas and Makes Them Real? Someone Who Finds New Ways to Interact, New Pathways to Deliver Emotion, New Ways to Connect? Someone Who Acts Like a Human, Not a Cog? Me?"

Yes.

The Poverty Mentality

If I give you something, it costs me what I gave you.

The more you have, the less I have.

The more I share, the more I lose.

How long have you had an approach to stuff or ideas or time that sounds like this? We've been taught it for a long time.

Digital goods call our bluff. If you read my e-book, we both win. If you share it, so do your friends. Attention is precious, and if you're willing to trade your attention for my idea, we both thrive.

But it goes far beyond that. When you give something away, you benefit more than the recipient does. The act of being generous makes you rich beyond measure, and as the goods or services spread through the community, everyone benefits.

But that's a hard thing to start doing, because you've been taught that what's yours is yours. If you don't have enough (and who does, say the marketers), then how can you possibly give away what you have? And yet, every day, successful people race to give away their expertise and to spread their ideas.

A Practical Reason to Become an Artist

Some people become artists because they have no choice. It is who they are and thus what they do. I'm not sure I can offer encouragement to these artists, as they already have everything they need to do their thing.

Others, perhaps you, hesitate. It doesn't seem like a reasonable way to support your family or make a difference in the world.

The role of art keeps changing.

For the longest time, ART (in capital letters) set you apart. Art was not a living, it wasn't practical, and it certainly wasn't a way to get rich or even change the world.

Over the last century or so, as capitalism has created huge surpluses of cash (or at least unevenly distributed piles of cash), the number of people willing to act as patrons has skyrocketed. So has the demand for souvenirs of art and art as an investment. As a result, art has moved from its own sphere into a sphere nestled right next to capitalism. The culture industry has turned artists of every kind (singers, playwrights, actors, painters) into millionaires and rock stars. But they were still of their own sphere.

Now, as the culture industry has infiltrated every industry (yes, there are designer steel mills, and yes, the interior design of a $20 million corporate jet is a huge part of the sale), artists have moved from the exterior of our economy to its center. Disney now licenses its images to egg farmers. Eggs now have Disney characters printed on the shells and you can scramble Mickey for breakfast. Everything from food to luggage to phones to pens to insurance forms is transformed by design and art and insight. If art is about humanity, and commerce has become about interactions (not stuff), then commerce is now about art, too.

The reason you might choose to embrace the artist within you now is that this is the path to (cue the ironic music) security.

When it is time for layoffs, the safest job belongs to the artist, the linchpin, the one who can't be easily outsourced or replaced.

Do You Need to Be an Artist to Market Tofu?

That's an interesting question. If you start with the assumption that an artist works with paint or clay or music, then this is a hard leap to make. If you believe that art is somehow separate from work, that it's a different sort of endeavor or a different sort of person, then it's almost impossible to imagine an artist marketing tofu.

I don't see it that way. I think art is the ability to change people with your work, to see things as they are and then create stories, images, and interactions that change the marketplace. So, yes, I do think you need to be an artist to market tofu, if you want to be any good at it.

Years ago, someone decided that there was a predictable, scalable, industrial solution to marketing. They asserted that coupons and incessant advertising, combined with distribution and aggressive pricing, were not only sufficient but essential to growing a brand. Now, as we've seen over the last decade, none of that by-the-book marketing shtick works so well. Now, it's more common to see the success of a brand like Jones Soda—not because founder Peter van Stolk followed the rules, but because he's an artist.

At its peak, the company was worth more than $300 million, and none of that value was generated by following the rule book.

Peter said, "I don't care what anybody does in the beverage industry. I really don't. They're going to do what they're going to do. We've got to do what we've got to do. You have to know what they're doing, but you don't have to follow what they're doing."

Is there art in being Jones? He broke every rule in the book. He put his customers' pictures on the bottle. He made mashed potato flavor. He answered the door when people came to visit. *People came to visit.* Do you think many people go visit the local Pepsi bottler?

Does that sound like a marketer to you? To me, it sounds like an artist. Perhaps the reason you can't name a beloved brand of tofu is that no artist has bothered to market it to you yet.

Would Shakespeare Blog?

Does the technology used by the artist appear on the scene to match what the artist needs, or do artists do their art with the tools that are available?

Shakespeare didn't invent plays; he used them. Salinger didn't invent the novel; he wrote a few. The technology existed before they got there.

I don't believe that you are born to do a certain kind of art, mainly because your genes have no idea what technology is going to be available to you. Cave painters, stone carvers, playwrights, chemists, quantum-mechanic mechanics—people do their art where they find it, not the other way around.

The art that you do when you interact with a customer, or when you create a new use of a traditional system or technology—it's still art. Our society has reorganized so that the answer to the question "where should I do art?" is now a long booklet, not a simple checklist of a few choices.

The Myth of Project-Specific Passion

In a pre-Internet world, where Amazon.com couldn't have existed, would Jeff Bezos be a nonpassionate lump? If Spike Lee hadn't found a camera, would he be sitting around, accepting the status quo?

Passion isn't project-specific. It's people-specific. Some people are hooked on passion, deriving their sense of self from the act of being passionate.

Perhaps your challenge isn't finding a better project or a better boss. Perhaps you need to get in touch with what it means to feel passionate. People with passion look for ways to make things happen.

The combination of passion and art is what makes someone a linchpin.

Touching Someone

Being open is art. Making a connection when it's not part of your job is a gift. You can say your lines and get away with it, or you can touch someone and make a difference in their lives forever.

This is risky and it's impossible to demand of someone. The decision to commit to the act is a personal one, a gift from the heart.

Certain sorts of art make us cry without embarrassment.

Understanding Gifts

When a magazine sends a photographer to take a picture of a celebrity, it is paying the photographer for a photo that's good enough to run in the magazine. The magazine is expecting a certain standard of photograph, and it's a commercial transaction.

Anything the photographer contributes above that is a gift. The inspiration, the lighting, or the surprise—that's a gift from the photographer to his client and to the readers of the magazine.

Annie Leibovitz built her career around this gift. She was hired to do celebrity photographs, but she kept pushing the limits. I would imagine that some of her shots were a hard sell to clients who believed that they were buying yesterday's version of Annie, not today's.

Over time, the gifts accrue and you have created a reputation.

There are two reasons to give a gift. I'm not so interested in the first one—reciprocity. You give a gift to someone because then he will owe you. This is manipulative and it's no way to build a career. Sociologist Marcel Mauss wrote about this a hundred years ago, and he argued that entire primitive societies were built around this reciprocity. The problem is that in capitalist societies, this instinct for reciprocity is easily misused.

The second reason, though, is fascinating. Gifts allow you to make art. Gifts are given with no reciprocity hoped for or even possible. I can't give the artist Chuck Close anything in return for the joy his low-resolution, hyperrealist paintings have given me. It's a gift with no possibility of reciprocity. This gives Chuck room—room to be in charge, room to experiment, room to find joy—because when he's painting, he's not punching a time clock or trying to please someone who bought his time. He's creating a gift.

My fundamental argument here is simple: In everything you do, it's possible to be an artist, at least a little bit. Not on demand, not in the same way each time, and not for everyone. But if you're willing to suspend your selfish impulses, you can give a gift to your customer or boss or coworker or a passerby. *And the gift is as much for you as it is for the recipient.*

Who Is It For?

Some artists work to change themselves. The process of making the art and the results produced are solely aimed at the creator. Whistling as you walk through the woods is a form of art, but you're not doing it hoping a squirrel will applaud.

Most of us, though, most of the time, make our art for an audience. We want to change someone else. We're seeking to make them happier, or more engaged, or a customer.

There are two reasons why it's vital to know whom you are working for. The first is that understanding your audience allows you to target your work and to get feedback that will help you do it better next time.

The other reason? Because it tells you whom to ignore.

It's impossible to make art for everyone. There are too many conflicting goals and there's far too much noise. Art for everyone is mediocre, bland, and ineffective.

If you don't pinpoint your audience, you end up making your art for the loudest, crankiest critics. And that's a waste. Instead, focus on the audience that *you* choose, and listen to them, to the exclusion of all others. Go ahead and make *this* sort of customer happy, and the other guys can go pound sand.

In the words of Ev Williams, founder of Blogger and Twitter,

The core thing would be just do something awesome. Try not to get caught up in the echo chamber. That is probably the toughest thing when you are trying to break out and do something original.

A lot of things are evolutionary, and it is easy to get caught up in what the geek subculture thinks. There's lots of valuable businesses that can be built there, but I think that is where a lot of people tend to spin their wheels, and I've been caught up there before. When I've had more successful things, I've thought, "Back to basics. What do I want? What do I want to see in the world?" And create that.

Ev and Twitter didn't succeed at first. People didn't get it. What's the point? Where's the business model? And then, once the word spread, Twitter became the fastest-growing communications medium in history. Not because it followed a model, but because it broke one.

Some artists create.

Some artists seek a patron, someone who will help them pay the bills while they do their work.

Some artists think they need a boss. Someone who will not only pay them, but also tell them what to do. The moment this happens, the artist is no longer an artist.

An artist's job is to change us. When you have a boss, your job is to please the boss, not to change her. It's okay to have someone you work for, someone who watches over you, someone who pays you. But the moment you treat that person like a boss, like someone in charge of your movements and your output, you are a cog, not an artist.

Nobody Cares How Hard You Worked

It's not an effort contest, it's an art contest. As customers, we care about ourselves, about how *we* feel, about whether a product or service or play or interaction changed us for the better.

Where it's made or how it's made or how difficult it was to make is sort of irrelevant. That's why emotional labor is so much more valuable than physical labor. Emotional labor changes the recipient, and we care about that.

Soft Gifts and the Conundrum for MBAs

This news is unsettling.

The future of your organization depends on motivated human beings selflessly contributing unasked-for gifts of emotional labor. And worse yet, the harder you work to quantify and manipulate this process, the more poorly it will work.

The most senior levels in organizations have wrestled with this situation for a long time. When you hire a vice president for business development, it's a given that he's not going to be your errand boy. You're not paying all this money for someone who will merely go down a checklist you've created and who will ask you before making any decisions. Of course not. It's his job to innovate, to create new opportunities, to connect with hard-to-reach people, and to follow the long line on the way to success.

As we go lower down the totem pole, though, management assumes that less pay = less humanity.

The facts belie that assumption. From the U.S. Army to the manager at your local McDonald's, it turns out that more humanity delivers better results. One of the most difficult tasks the military had in Iraq was to teach soldiers how to treat Iraqi civilians as potential partners, how to vary from the stated mission of the day, how to be human in the face of huge unknown danger. It's easy to teach someone how to fire a missile, but very difficult to take risks in the face of fear.

The digitization of work (measurement, Internet connection, mechanization) makes typical MBAs very happy. This is the sort of thing you can put in a spreadsheet. The challenge is that all your competitors are using the same spreadsheet, so your opportunity for quantum growth and significant market advantage is tiny.

The easier it is to quantify, the less it's worth.

The Job Versus Your Art

The job is what you do when you are told what to do. The job is showing up at the factory, following instructions, meeting spec, and being managed.

Someone can always do your job a little better or faster or cheaper than you can.

The job might be difficult, it might require skill, but it's a job.

Your art is what you do when no one can tell you exactly how to do it. Your art is the act of taking personal responsibility, challenging the status quo, and changing people.

I call the process of doing your art "the work." It's possible to have a job and do the work, too. In fact, that's how you become a linchpin.

The job is not the work.

Can Your Work Become Your Art?

Can the time you spend at work be the place you give gifts, create connections, invent, and find joy?

What has to change for that to be true—does something external need to change, or is it an internal decision?

I've found people in every job you can imagine doing art. There are waiters and writers and musicians and doctors and nurses and lawyers who find art in their work. The job is not your work; what you do with your heart and soul is the work.

A Few Questions About Emotional Labor

Are you indispensable at home? Would it fall apart without you?

What about at work?

Why are you easily replaceable at one venue but not the other?

Are you charming when you go on a date or meet a handsome guy at a party?

But not at a meeting at work?

I'm wondering why we're so easily able to expend emotional labor off the job, but uncomfortable expending the same energy on the job.

Artists Are Optimists

The reason is simple: artists have the chance to make things better.

Other people often make the choice to be victims. They can be the flotsam and jetsam tossed by the waves of circumstance. Until they make the choice to be artists, they sadly float along.

Artists understand that they have the power, through gifts, innovation, and love, to create a new story, one that's better than the old one.

Optimism is the most important human trait, because it allows us to evolve our ideas, to improve our situation, and to hope for a better tomorrow. And all artists have this optimism, because artists can honestly say that they are working to make things better.

This is why organizations under pressure often crack. All parties can see that their current system isn't working, but they're unable to embrace a new one because they're certain that it won't turn out perfectly, that it can't be as good as what they have now. Organizations under pressure are stuck because their pain makes it hard for them to believe in the future.

Optimism is for artists, change agents, linchpins, and winners. Whining and fear, on the other hand, are largely self-fulfilling prophecies in organizations under stress.

The Passion to Spread

Passion is caring enough about your art that you will do almost anything to give it away, to make it a gift, to change people.

Part of the passion is having the persistence and resilience to change both your art and the way you deliver it. Passion for your art also means having a passion for *spreading* your art. This means being willing to surrender elements that you are in love with in order to help the other parts thrive and spread. And at the same time, passion means having enough connection to your art that you're not willing to surrender the parts that truly matter.

It's a paradox, of course. In order to be true to your art, you must sacrifice the part of it that hinders the spread of your art.

Deciding what to leave out and what to insist on is part of your art. One author I know is willing to watch his books sit unsold, because that's a better outcome to him than changing the essence of what he's written. He has passion for his craft, but no real passion for spreading his ideas. And if the ideas don't spread, if no gift is received, then there is no art, only effort. When an artist stops work before his art is received, his work is unfulfilled.

Fear of Art

How powerful is the art you are able to create? Do genes and upbringing and cultural imperatives force you to surrender in your quest to deliver art that matters?

Was Harper Lee born to write *To Kill a Mockingbird*? Is there some combination of genetic gifts and parental nudging that created the perfect opportunity for her to generate such a monumental piece of art?

Let's go back to the beginning of this book.

Everyone, every single person, has been a genius at least once. Everyone has winged it, invented, and created their way out of a jam at least once.

If you can do it once, you can do it again.

Art, at least art as I define it, is the intentional act of using your humanity to create a change in another person. How and where you do that art is a cultural choice in the moment. No one wrote novels a thousand years ago. No one made videos thirty years ago. No one Twittered poetry three years ago.

There's no doubt that certain sorts of art are easier to create. A warm smile to a stranger on an airplane at the right moment is an artistic endeavor that's fairly easy for most of us to muster. Directing an Academy Award–winning film, on the other hand, is reserved for a select few. I'll accept the fact that great novelists are born *and* made. But I don't believe that you need to be an outlier to be an artist.

I'm not so interested in pushing you to become a brilliant filmmaker. I'm very passionate about exploring why you are so afraid about creating art that is actually within your grasp.

Why didn't you speak up at the meeting yesterday? When you had a chance to reach out and interact with a co-worker in a way that would have changed everything, what held you back? That proposal for a new project that's been sitting on your hard drive for a year . . .

Why aren't all waiters amazingly great at being waiters?

I think it's fear, and I think we're even afraid to talk about this sort of fear. Fear of art. Of being laughed at. Of standing out and of standing for something.

Now, though, the economy is forcing us to confront this fear. The economy is ruthlessly punishing the fearful, and increasing the benefits to the few who are brave enough to create art and generous enough to give it away.

THE RESISTANCE

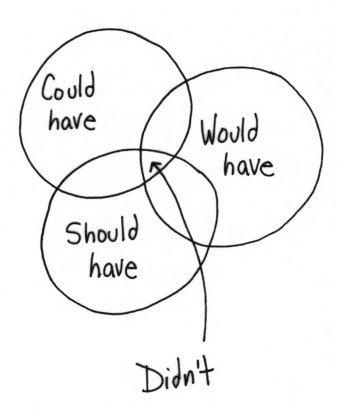

"Real Artists Ship"

When Steve Jobs said that, he was calling the bluff of a recalcitrant engineer who couldn't let go of some code. But this three-word mantra goes deeper than that. Poet Bruce Ario said, "Creativity is an instinct to produce."

And that's the art we care about.

Andy Hertzfeld, one of the fathers of the Mac, contributed to a diary about the launch of the original Mac, the computer that changed everything. He wrote, "The sun had already risen and the software team finally began to scatter and go home to collapse. We weren't sure if we were finished or not, and it felt really strange to have nothing to do after working so hard for so long. Instead of going home, Donn Denman and I sat on a couch in the lobby in a daze and watched the accounting and marketing people trickling into work around 7:30 a.m. or so. We must have been quite a sight; everybody could tell that we had been there all night (actually, I hadn't been home or showered for three days)." In that moment, Andy felt like an artist. He had shipped.

Artists don't think outside the box, because outside the box there's a vacuum. Outside of the box there are no rules, there is no reality. You have nothing to interact with, nothing to work against. If you set out to do something way outside the box (designing a time machine, or using liquid nitrogen to freeze Niagara Falls), then you'll never be able to do the real work of art. You can't ship if you're far outside the box.

Artists think along the edges of the box, because that's where things get done. That's where the audience is, that's where the means of production are available, and that's where you can make an impact.

Shipping isn't focused on producing a masterpiece (but all masterpieces get shipped). I've produced more than a hundred books (most didn't sell very well), but if I hadn't, I'd never have had the chance to write this one. Picasso painted more than a thousand paintings, and you can probably name three of them.

As we'll see, the greatest shortage in our society is an instinct to produce. To create solutions and hustle them out the door. To touch the humanity inside and connect to the humans in the marketplace.

The Contradiction Between Shipping and Changing the World

Sometimes, shipping feels like a compromise. You set out to make a huge difference, to create art that matters and to do your best work.

Then a deadline arrives and you have to cut it short. Is shipping that important?

I think it is. I think the discipline of shipping is essential in the long-term path to becoming indispensable. While some artists manage to work for years or decades and actually ship something important, far more often we find the dreams of art shattered by the resistance. We give in to the fear and our art ends up lying in a box somewhere, unseen.

When you first adopt the discipline of shipping, your work will appear to suffer. There's no doubt that another hour, day, or week would have added some needed polish. But over time—rather quickly, actually—you'll see that shipping becomes part of the art and shipping makes it work. *Saturday Night Live* goes on each week, ready or not. The show is live, and it's on Saturday. No screwing around about shipping. There are no do-overs, no stalls, no delays. Sometimes the show suffers, of course, but on balance, it's the shipping (built right into the name) that actually makes the show work.

Not shipping on behalf of your goal of changing the world is often a symptom of the resistance. Call its bluff, ship always, and *then* change the world.

What It Means to Ship

The only purpose of starting is to finish, and while the projects we do are never really finished, they must ship. Shipping means hitting the *publish* button on your blog, showing a presentation to the sales team, answering the phone, selling the muffins, sending out your references. Shipping is the collision between your work and the outside world. The French refer to *esprit d'escalier*, the clever comeback that you think of a few minutes after the moment has passed. This is unshipped insight, and it doesn't count for much.

Shipping something out the door, doing it regularly, without hassle, emergency, or fear—this is a rare skill, something that makes you indispensable.

Why is shipping so difficult? I think there are two challenges and one reason:

The challenges:

1. Thrashing
2. Coordination

And the reason:

The resistance.

Thrashing

Steve McConnell helped us understand how poorly timed thrashing sabotages every failed software project. It turns out that the problem extends far beyond software.

Any project worth doing involves invention, inspiration, and at least a little bit of making stuff up. Traditionally, we start with an inkling, adding more and more detail as we approach the ship date. And the closer we get to shipping, the more thrashing occurs. Thrashing is the apparently productive brainstorming and tweaking we do for a project as it develops. Thrashing might mean changing the user interface or rewriting an introductory paragraph. Sometimes thrashing is merely a tweak; other times it involves major surgery.

Thrashing is essential. The question is: when to thrash?

In the typical amateur project, all the thrashing is near the end. The closer we get to shipping, the more people get involved, the more meetings we have, the more likely the CEO wants to be involved. And why not? What's the point of getting involved early when you can't see what's already done and your work will probably be redone anyway?

The point of getting everyone involved early is simple: thrash late and you won't ship. Thrash late and you introduce bugs. Professional creators thrash early. The closer the project gets to completion, the fewer people see it and the fewer changes are permitted.

Every software project that has missed its target date (every single one) is a victim of late thrashing. The creators didn't have the discipline to force all the thrashing to the beginning. They fell victim to the resistance.

Coordination

Handshakes.

How many handshakes do you need to introduce three people? Only three. Ishita, meet Susan. Susan, meet Clay. Clay, meet Ishita.

Four people need twice as many, six.

And five people? Ten.

Coordinating teams of people becomes exponentially more difficult as the group gets larger. And for important projects in an organization with something to lose, the group pushes to get larger. People with something at stake (and we all believe we have something at stake) want to get involved in the really good projects, mostly because we're afraid that everyone else will screw it up and we'll get blamed.

So projects stall as they thrash. Nine women can't have a baby in one month, no matter how closely they coordinate their work.

The reason that start-ups almost always defeat large companies in the rush to market is simple: start-ups have fewer people to coordinate, less thrashing, and more linchpins per square foot. They can't afford anything else and they have less to lose.

There are two solutions to the coordination problem, and both of them make people uncomfortable, because both challenge our resistance.

1. Relentlessly limit the number of people allowed to thrash. That means you need formal procedures for excluding people, even well-meaning people with authority. And you need secrecy. If you have a choice between being surprised (and watching a great project ship on time) or being involved (and participating in the late launch of a mediocre project), which do you want? You must pick one or the other.

2. Appoint one person (a linchpin) to run it. Not to co-run it or to lead a task force or to be on the committee. One person, a human being, runs it. Her name on it. Her decisions.

Get scared early, not late. Be brave early, not late. Thrash now, not later. It's too expensive to thrash later.

The Resistance: Your Lizard Brain

The lizard brain is hungry, scared, angry, and horny.

The lizard brain only wants to eat and be safe.

The lizard brain will fight (to the death) if it has to, but would rather run away. It likes a vendetta and has no trouble getting angry.

The lizard brain cares what everyone else thinks, because status in the tribe is essential to its survival.

A squirrel runs around looking for nuts, hiding from foxes, listening for predators, and watching for other squirrels. The squirrel does this because that's all it can do. All the squirrel has is a lizard brain.

The only correct answer to "Why did the chicken cross the road?" is "Because its lizard brain told it to." Wild animals are wild because the only brain they possess is a lizard brain.

The lizard brain is not merely a concept. It's real, and it's living on the top of your spine, fighting for your survival. But, of course, survival and success are not the same thing.

The lizard brain is the reason you're afraid, the reason you don't do all the art you can, the reason you don't ship when you can. The lizard brain is the source of the resistance.

The Daemon and the Resistance

Your mind, the thing that drives you crazy and makes you special, has two distinct sections, the daemon and the resistance.

The daemon is the source of great ideas, groundbreaking insights, generosity, love, connection, and kindness.

The resistance spends all its time insulating the world from our daemon. The resistance lives inside the lizard brain.

I first heard about the daemon when Elizabeth Gilbert talked about hers at TED (you can watch the video at www.ted.org). Then I read the source of her talk: Lewis Hyde's take on it in *The Gift*.

Daemon is a Greek term (the Romans called it a "genius"). The Greeks believed that the daemon was a separate being inside each of us. The genius living inside of us would struggle to express itself in art or writing or some other endeavor. When the genius felt like showing up, great stuff happened. If not, you were sort of out of luck.

Elizabeth warns us that the life of the writer is a life that could end up on "the scrap heap of broken dreams with your mouth filled with the bitter ash of failure." Why do creative ventures threaten our mental health, she wonders. Why is there writer's block but no chemical engineering block? Artistry, it seems, always leads to anguish. This anguish is caused by the clash between the daemon and the resistance. Society pushes artists to *be* geniuses, as opposed to encouraging artists to allow the genius within to flourish. Different tasks.

Anguish? Sure. The conflict between your ideas and the outside world. More important, the chasm between the part of you that wants to be safe and invisible, and your daemon, which is demanding to speak to the world.

Every time you find yourself following the manual instead of writing the manual, you're avoiding the anguish and giving in to the resistance.

Artists write down what the daemon says. In Elizabeth's words, "I showed up for my part of the job." The daemon is the artist inside of you; your work is just to allow it to do its thing.

This is far more difficult than it sounds. In his classic book *The War of Art*, Steven Pressfield calls our inability to easily free the daemon "the resistance."

Pressfield says that the daemon's enemy is the resistance. Your lizard brain, the part that the daemon has no control over, is working overtime to get you to shut up, sit down, and do your (day) job. It will invent stories, illnesses, emergencies, and distractions in order to keep the genius bottled up. The resistance is afraid. Afraid of what will happen to you (and to it) if the ideas get out, if your gifts are received, if the magic happens.

You know the resistance is there. You've felt it. Perhaps you didn't have a name for it, or recognize all the symptoms, but you can be sure that it is a part of you.

I've seen it wreck people, teams, and corporations. The resistance is nefarious and clever. It creates diseases, procrastination, and most especially, rationalization. Lots and lots of rationalization, some of which you might be experiencing right now.

The resistance has been around for a million years and the lizard brain will not give up easily. While the neocortex (that's where your daemon lives) is much newer from an evolutionary standpoint, it's not stronger. Given the chance, the lizard brain will shut you down and the resistance will win.

The resistance almost beat Elizabeth Gilbert. After selling millions and millions of copies of *Eat, Pray, Love*, the resistance was afraid of what her next book might do to her career. "People treat me like I'm doomed. Aren't you afraid you'll never be able to top that?" she said. The lizard brain was loud and angry and afraid and it set out to defeat her.

Elizabeth wrote her next book, right on time, and brought it to a copy shop to print out the first draft. Standing there, she read it. "It was different from just the anxiety and insecurities that you feel when you're writing something," she said. "It was nondebatable." The lizard brain won. She threw out an entire book, junked it, trashed it, missed her deadline and started over. More than a year's work gone.

Fortunately, she has a new book on the way. She persisted and found another way to beat the lizard. But it's clear that no matter what sort of creative work you're doing, no matter how successful or acclaimed you are, the lizard will seek you out and probably find you. What happens after that is up to you.

How the Resistance Evolved

Actually, it got here first.

The first part of our brain, the part that shows up first in the womb, the part that was there a million years ago—that's our lizard brain. The lizard brain is in charge of fight or flight, of anger, and of survival. That's all we used to need, and even now, when there's an emergency, the lizard brain is still in charge.

There are several small parts of your brain near the end of your spinal cord responsible for survival and other wild-animal traits. The whole thing is called the basal ganglia, and there are two almond-shaped bits in everyone's brain. Scientists call these the amygdala, and this mini-brain apparently takes over whenever you are angry, afraid, aroused, hungry, or in search of revenge.

It's only recently that our brains evolved to allow big thoughts, generosity, speech, consciousness, and yes, art. When you look at a picture of the brain, the new part is what you see: the neocortex. That's the wrinkly gray part on the outside. It's big, but it's weak. In the face of screaming resistance from the amygdala, the rest of your brain is helpless. It freezes and surrenders. The lizard takes over and tries to protect itself.

The challenge, then, is to create an environment where the lizard snoozes. You can't beat it, so you must seduce it. One part of your brain worries about survival and anger and lust. The rest of it creates civilization.

This is part metaphor, part biology. The lizard brain is here to keep you alive; the rest of your brain merely makes you a happy, successful, connected member of society.

So the two parts duke it out. And when put on alert, the lizard brain wins, every time, unless you've established new habits and better patterns—patterns that keep the lizard at bay.

(Evolving a Brain That Could Create Civilization)

Quick oversimplified biology lesson: Here are four of the major systems in your brain. (Note: "system" is more of a conceptual hook for understanding what happens as opposed to a biological truth or hard wiring.) As you go down the list, each system becomes more civilized but less powerful:

1. **Brain Stem**—breathing and other unconscious survival functions
2. **Limbic System**—the lizard brain. Anger and revenge and sex and fear.
3. **Cerebellum**—coordination and motor control
4. **Cerebrum**—the newest and most sophisticated part of our brain, and also the one that is always overruled by the other three parts.

There are four lobes to the cerebrum, and their functions are the stuff to be proud of:

Frontal Lobe: reasoning, planning, parts of speech, movement, problem solving

Parietal Lobe: movement, orientation, recognition, perception of stimuli

Occipital Lobe: eyesight (and the essential, overlooked, and under-rated orbitofrontal cortex, which integrates the lizard brain with your rational mind)

Temporal Lobe: hearing, memory, and speech

You can't give a speech while drowning. You can't fall in love while having a heart attack. You can't write a sonnet at the same time you're vomiting from being on a roller coaster.

The metaphor goes like this: the older a brain system is on the evolutionary scale (and the closer to the brain stem), the more power it has to suspend the actions of the younger systems. And the lizard brain within the limbic system is the loudest example of this metaphor. You rarely have a heart attack (I hope) and you probably won't get so dizzy that you fall down, but your amygdala regularly suspends all civilized activity within your brain and takes over, putting you into lockdown.

More than fifty years ago, physician and neuroscientist Paul MacLean did research at Yale and at the National Institute of Mental Health. He laid out what he called triune theory, which led to the thinking behind the lizard brain. Combine this with Antonio Damasio's work in understanding the role of the orbitofrontal cortex in integrating the lizard with the more rational parts of the mind and you can see the never-ending struggle and collaboration the two parts of your brain create.

The Man with Two Brains

That would be me. You too, obviously.

Why do people do things that are self-destructive? Why work on a paper for a week but never save it or back it up? Why do entrepreneurs get so close to success and then sabotage all the work that they've done in a moment of fear?

We mess up precisely because of the "we." There are two, not one, voices in our head, and one of them is closer to the spine and the chemicals that generate our emotions than the other. So it's often in charge.

Neurologists studying brain disorders have discovered remarkable behaviors. In one case, a woman suffered from severe short-term memory loss. Anything more than five minutes old never happened. Every morning, she woke up with no recollection of anything less than a year or two ago. She knew her name and her distant past, but nothing recent. (Similar to the plot of the great movie *Memento*.)

Each day, she'd visit her doctor. He would shake her hand, reintroduce himself, and they would start over. One day, in a fairly unethical experiment, he put a thumbtack in his hand. When they shook hands, she was pinched. It hurt. He explained to her what he had done, and of course, an hour later she had forgotten all about it.

The next day, though, when the doctor extended his hand, she flinched. How did she know about the thumbtack? Her short-term memory was clearly gone. She wasn't faking. And yet, she remembered enough to avoid the pain.

This was her amygdala at work. It has its own memory, its own survival system in place. The lizard brain stands by, jumping into action whenever basic survival needs are at stake. And when it is aroused, the other part of our brain stands little chance, particularly if we haven't trained it for these events.

And so, the conflict. The conflict between what feels good now and what we ought to do. This explains how someone with throat cancer can persist in smoking, or how an obese person who clearly knows better can persist in eating "just one more doughnut." In the face of greed or fear from the amygdala, an untrained person surrenders.

Sales resistance? Why is it that some salespeople put in years of training, hours of effort, thousands of dollars in travel expenses and then leave without the sale, while others push through to reach the last (profitable) part and walk out with the order? That's the two brains again, the amygdala fleeing the moment that it feels threatened.

Weak managers? Why is it that so many bosses shy away from useful criticism or substantive leadership? Why is it so easy to hide behind an office door or a title instead of looking people in the eye and making a difference? Same answer. The amygdala resists looking people in the eye, because doing so is threatening and exposes it to risk.

Deadlines? Surely you know someone who is late all the time. Someone who can't deliver anything of value unless they've stalled so much they've created an urgency, an emergency that requires mind-blowing effort and adrenaline to deliver. This is not efficient or reliable behavior, and yet they persist. The reason is simple: they can't push through the common fear of completion unless they can create a greater fear of total failure. The lizard brain is impulsive, but for these people, it's also capable of choosing the greater risk and avoiding it.

In fact, if we go down the list of behaviors that are highly valued because of their scarcity, almost all of them are related to bringing a conscious and generous mind to the work, instead of indulging our lizard brain's reflexes of fear, revenge, and conquest.

(Eye Contact and the Lizard Brain)

The Rotterdam Zoo now distributes special eyeglasses for visitors to the gorilla area.

The glasses are sort of like the 3D glasses from the movies, except that they don't change what you see. They change what the gorilla sees. They have a picture painted on them of your eyes looking to the side.

This way, when you are near the gorillas, it doesn't look like you're making eye contact with them. Which is threatening. Which freaks the gorillas out and has led to attacks.

Eye contact, all by itself, is enough to throw your lizard brain into a tizzy. Imagine how scary it must be to set out to do something that will get you noticed, or perhaps even criticized.

There's a reason that the number-one fear reported by most people is public speaking. Public speaking is one of the worst things the lizard brain can imagine.

It's Difficult to Reason with the Lizard

It's hard to talk an alcoholic out of his addiction. Hard to get a teenager to see the consequences of his impulsive actions. Nearly impossible to talk an angry CEO down from a revenge rage. Last year, a CEO I know was doing a demo for an investor. As part of the demo, he clicked over to a partner's Web site. There, in living color, in front of the investors, was an off-color, not-safe-for-work photograph.

The CEO flipped. For three days, he spent virtually all of his time and money trying to void his company's contract with the partner. All hands on deck. No compromises. Destroy!

What a waste. He cost his company tons of time and money and goodwill, all to fix a problem that was too late to fix.

The lizard isn't listening and the lizard doesn't care.

The only hope for our species is that the rest of the brain, the civilized part, will care so deeply about positive outcomes that it will organize to avoid the lizard, and will invest in systems that make the resistance less powerful.

The Resistance at Work

"See, I told you it would never work."

You've presented your great idea, and people hate it. They ridicule you and threaten you and tell you to go away.

Your subconscious speaks up. It says something like, "You should have listened to me. You really blew it." Or perhaps it says, "I knew you shouldn't have done that."

Who, exactly, is "you"? And whom is this voice addressing?

The voice in your head has revealed the resistance. It is trying to teach the daemon a lesson, encouraging it to be more careful next time. The lizard hates your genius, and tries to stamp it out. When you hear this dialogue, don't listen to it. Remember that it serves as proof of the resistance, and guard yourself even more diligently to ignore it.

The Lizard Goes to School

Of course, the resistance loves school. If school is about obedience, then you can be soothed by thinking that more obedience is better work, and the resistance is fine with that. If school is about fitting in, the resistance happily agrees. If school is about postponing the day you have to stand up in front of the world and put yourself at risk, the resistance would like to stay there forever.

It's the lizard brain that tells you that you're not qualified, that your degree isn't advanced enough, that you didn't go to a good enough school. It's the lizard that tells you not to apply to a great school, because you don't deserve to get in. And it's the lizard that cares deeply about grades, and not a bit about art or leadership or connection.

The Lizard Goes to Work

You work with people who are totally at the mercy of the resistance. They assist the devil by being his advocate in meetings. They follow the rule book, even parts you didn't know about. They love what worked before and fear what might be coming.

Sites like lifehacker.com are stuffed with time-saving, productivity-enhancing tools. In general, your nervous co-workers avoid these tools, because being more productive just gets them that much closer to having to actually do something, to ship something new out the door. And surprisingly, the folks who are always busy filling up notebooks with tips and tasks are just as afraid. Looking busy is not the same as fighting the resistance. Being productive at someone else's task list is not the same as making your own map.

The Hard Part About Losing

The reason the resistance persists in slowing you down and prevents you from putting your heart and soul and art into your work is simple: *you might fail.*

Of course you might. In fact, you will. Not all the time, certainly, but more than you'd like.

And when you fail, then what?

My friend JP lost her job. She's amazing at what she does, she deserves to be promoted, not fired. She brings everything she has to work, every day, and they were so lucky to have her. But these dolts, they fired her.

Some people would take that as a slap, a cut deep into their soul, a message that they ought to back off, stop trying, and care less.

JP did the opposite. First, she realized that they made a bad decision, not that she did a bad job (good call). And second, she quickly understood that if she let the resistance stand up and say, "I told you so," she'd be giving in. Give in to the resistance and you might never recover.

Successful people are successful for one simple reason: they think about failure differently.

Successful people learn from failure, but the lesson they learn is a different one. They don't learn that they shouldn't have tried in the first place, and they don't learn that they are always right and the world is wrong and they don't learn that they are losers. They learn that the tactics they used didn't work or that the person they used them on didn't respond.

You become a winner because you're good at losing. The hard part about losing is that you might permit it to give strength to the resistance, that you might believe that you don't deserve to win, that you might, in some dark corner of your soul, give up.

Don't.

Seeking Out Discomfort

Going out of your way to find uncomfortable situations isn't natural, but it's essential.

The resistance seeks comfort. The resistance wants to hide. At work, we spend hours (and millions of dollars) seeking a place we can defend, a market position and sinecure we can feel safe in. Corporations watch their stocks soar when they can describe a comfortable market niche that will generate profits for years to come. College professors often pick the profession because of the comfort that tenure brings. Salespeople embrace the script because using one is more comfortable than engaging with the prospect. Bosses resist giving direct and useful feedback to employees because it's momentarily uncomfortable.

The road to comfort is crowded and it rarely gets you there. Ironically, it's those who seek out discomfort that are able to make a difference and find their footing.

Inevitably, we exaggerate just how uncomfortable we are. An uncomfortable seat on a long airplane flight begins to feel like a open wound. This exaggeration makes it even more likely that embracing the discomfort that others fear is likely to deliver real rewards.

Discomfort brings engagement and change. Discomfort means you're doing something that others were unlikely to do, because they're busy hiding out in the comfortable zone. When your uncomfortable actions lead to success, the organization rewards you and brings you back for more.

Developing Plan B

Well-meaning friends and advisers never hesitate to reach out to artists. They suggest we have a backup plan, something to fall back on if the art thing doesn't work out so well.

You've probably guessed what happens when you have a great backup plan: You end up settling for the backup. As soon as you say, "I'll try my best," instead of "I will," you've opened the door for the lizard.

The resistance desperately seeks to sabotage your art. A well-defined backup plan is sabotage waiting to happen. Why push through the dip, why take the risk, why blow it all when there's the comfortable alternative instead? The people who break through usually have nothing to lose, and they almost never have a backup plan.

Where Are All the Good Ideas?

When someone says to me, "I don't have any good ideas . . . I'm just not good at that," I ask them, "Do you have any bad ideas?"

Nine times out of ten, the answer is no. Finding good ideas is surprisingly easy once you deal with the problem of finding bad ideas. All the creativity books in the world aren't going to help you if you're unwilling to have lousy, lame, and even dangerously bad ideas.

The resistance abhors bad ideas. It would rather have you freeze up and invent nothing than take a risk and have some portion of your output be laughable. Every creative person I know generates a slew of laughable ideas for every good one. Some people (like me) need to create two slews for every good one.

One way to become creative is to discipline yourself to generate bad ideas. The worse the better. Do it a lot and magically you'll discover that some good ones slip through.

You Don't Need More Genius.
You Need Less Resistance.

The resistance is the voice in your head telling you to use bullets in your PowerPoint slides, because that's what the boss wants. It's the voice that tells you to leave controversial ideas out of the paper you're writing, because the teacher won't like them. The resistance pushes relentlessly for you to fit in.

In difficult economic times, the resistance explains that we'd better get a steady job, because the world is fraught with uncertainty and this is no time to do something crazy like starting a company. And in great times, of course, the resistance persuades us not to start a company because competition is fierce and hey, salaries are high. "Don't be stupid," it says.

The resistance wants you to check your e-mail now, because something great may have shown up (or more likely, something horrible). No time to sketch out a new product . . . why are you always dreaming . . . we need to focus on getting that conference call scheduled.

The resistance is so tenacious that it encourages you to speak up and drag down anyone around you with the temerity to dream. "Sure, Bob's presentation was okay, but did he make the quarterly numbers? We have stockholders to please."

The devil's advocate is actually a card-carrying member of the resistance. There are entire corporations filled with people like this, people who work overtime to stamp out any insight or art. In their quest for job safety, they are laying the groundwork for their own demise.

The most pernicious thing (from an author's point of view) is that the lizard hates it when you read books like this one.

Uncomfortable with Permission

When you started reading this book, did it make you squirm a bit when I called you a genius?

A lot of people are uncomfortable with that sort of permission, authority, or leverage. If you're a genius, after all, then you need to deliver genius-quality results.

You've almost certainly been brainwashed to believe that you aren't a genius, that you're working at the appropriate level, earning what you're supposed to earn, and doing what you're supposed to do. And some of that brainwashing has been consensual, because your resistance sort of likes low expectations.

Once you've given a name to the resistance and you know what its voice sounds like, it's a lot easier to embrace the fact that you actually *are* a genius. The part of you that wants to deny this is the resistance. The rest of you understands that you're as capable as the next guy of an insight, invention, or connection that makes a difference.

Freedom Feeds the Resistance

Cog workers have very little freedom at their jobs. Their output is measured, their tasks are described, and they either produce or are fired.

So, cog workers don't wrestle much with resistance. If you go to your job at a chicken slaughterhouse, you're going to behead chickens all day, or you won't have a job tomorrow. It's lousy work, sure, but the lizard brain isn't often aroused while doing it. Follow the rules, repeat.

The freedom of the new kind of work (which most of us do, most of the time) is that the tasks are vague and difficult to measure. We can waste an hour surfing the 'Net because no one knows if surfing the 'Net is going to help us make progress or connections.

This freedom is great, because it means no one is looking over your shoulder; no one is using a stopwatch on you.

This freedom is a pox, because it's an opening for the resistance. Freedom like this makes it easy to hide, easy to find excuses, easy to do very little.

Some Classical Musicians Aren't Artists

Classical music is a fascinating example of the resistance and its role in our corporate system, because the rules are so clear and the results are so easy to measure.

For ten or twenty years, music students are taught (while living in fear of the resistance) to play things as written. There's a score, there's a sound, play the notes and be part of the team.

So we churn out very good second violinists and very competent timpani players. We have a surplus of them, in fact, and that's why it's a dicey way to make a living, with only a few talented (and lucky) musicians making good money or holding steady jobs. Often guest conductors don't even know the names of the people who make up the bulk of the orchestra.

One conductor I know travels the world giving corporate performances, hiring competent musicians with little notice in each city. He pays them hardly anything, because there are so many to choose from. The surplus of cookie-cutter musicians has destroyed any hope for the creation of value and a better-than-fair wage.

And yet . . .

And yet it's Yo-Yo Ma and Ben Zander and Gustavo Dudamel who are in demand, who make great money, and who are having all the fun. These are the guys who don't fit in, who don't follow the score, who know the rules but break them. They are artists. Many others have been indoctrinated by the system and frightened by the resistance into following instructions.

Standardized News

Journalism is another great example, because it's easy to glamorize the profession and easy for people to confuse the value of the final product (honest, insightful news reporting) with the cost of making that product. Media economist Robert Picard said,

> Well-paying employment requires that workers possess unique skills, abilities, and knowledge. It also requires that the labor must be non-commoditized. Unfortunately, journalistic labor has become commoditized. Most journalists share the same skill sets and the same approaches to stories, seek out the same sources, ask similar questions, and produce relatively similar stories. . . .
>
> Across the news industry, processes and procedures for news gathering are guided by standardized news values, producing standardized stories in standardized formats that are presented in standardized styles. The result is extraordinary sameness and minimal differentiation.
>
> It is clear that journalists do not want to be in the contemporary labor market, much less the highly competitive information market. They prefer to justify the value they create in the moral philosophy terms of instrumental value. Most believe that what they do is so intrinsically good and that they should be compensated to do it even if it doesn't produce revenue.

This is precisely what your organization is facing. Over time, drip by drip, year by year, the manual was written, the procedures were set, and people were hired to follow the rules. The organization gets extremely efficient at producing a certain output a certain way . . . and then competition or change or technology arrives and the old rules aren't particularly useful, the old efficiencies not so profitable.

In the face of a threat like this, the natural reaction is to try to become more efficient. Run fewer pages, do some strategic layoffs (lay off the weird outliers or the expensive old-timers). *The New York Times* recently responded by making their Sunday magazine smaller and replacing the typeface with one that crams more letters on each page.

Of course, this isn't the answer. Doing more of what you were doing, but more obediently, more measurably, and more averagely (is that a word?), will not solve the problem, it will make it worse. Making the resistance happy is not the same as succeeding. What do you say to your board of directors? You don't scare them with bold plans, you hunker down, give in to the lizard, and die slowly instead.

The Huffington Post, which soon will make more money than any newspaper in the country, threw out the rules. They have no printing plants, no revered style manual, not even a fancy building. Instead, they're staffing up with artists and change makers. If they succeed, it will be because they confronted the resistance.

"This Might Work"

You'd think that the biggest self-doubt would be that something you're working on might fail. And no doubt, many of us lie awake, filled with anxiety about big failures. Consider the argument that it's just as likely you hold back out of fear that something might work.

If it works, then you have to do it. Then you have to do it again. Then you have to top it. If it works, your world changes. There are new threats and new challenges and new risks. That's world-class frightening.

Duncan Hines built an empire that ended up being worth more than half a billion dollars when his partner finally died in 1993. When Hines was building his brand, he used nothing more than some postage stamps and a printing press. He was a door-to-door salesman who wrote a restaurant guide in his spare time.

It took at least ten years for Duncan Hines the man to become Duncan Hines the world-famous brand. Any time during those ten years, a better-organized, better-capitalized competitor could have wiped him out. Your grandparents could have done it. By that time, there was no doubt that what Hines was doing was going to work. He wasn't hiding his success, it was well chronicled. No, the risk for someone challenging him was that he might compete and actually win. That would change everything.

Fast forward fifty years and the very same inclinations and fears are at work. Why didn't the countless smart people running newspapers around the country see what was happening online and actually organize to take advantage of it? Why is Carolyn Reidy, the publisher of fabled book publisher Simon & Schuster, fighting against the Kindle tooth and nail?

The temptation to sabotage the new thing is huge, precisely because the new thing might work.

When Did the Resistance Take Over Your Life?

When you were a kid, beautiful art—questions, curiosity, and spontaneity—poured out of you. The resistance was only starting to figure out how to shout out the art coming from the rest of your brain. Then, thanks to disorganized hazing by friends, raised eyebrows from the family, and well-meaning, well-organized, but toxic rules at school, the resistance gained in strength.

Do you think it's an accident that the powers that be wanted the disobedient and creative part of your brain to sit down and shut up?

If you were unlucky enough to get a job in a factory, the resistance was officially put in charge. I've met executives at insurance companies, assembly-line workers, and customer service people who have the resistance so thoroughly entrenched they don't even realize it's there. For them, this is normal. They think they're being mature and realistic when they're actually cowering in fear.

Our society has carved out some professions where one is expected to be creative for a living. And yet, even in the movies, visual arts, and book publishing, the systems we have in place make it far easier to fake the act of creativity than to actually embrace it. The art each of us is capable of creating is relentlessly whittled away. Ask editors and agents in these industries for horror stories, and they're sure to tell you about someone who "went a little too far" and ended up getting laughed out of a job. The thing is, it's always the same story about the same guy, because examples are few and far between.

Our economy has reached a logical conclusion. The race to make average stuff for average people in huge quantities is almost over. We're hitting an asymptote, a natural ceiling for how cheaply and how fast we can deliver uninspired work.

Becoming more average, more quick, and more cheap is not as productive as it used to be.

Manufacturing a box that can play music went from $10,000 for a beautiful Edison Victrola to $2,000 for a home stereo to $300 for a Walkman to $200 for an iPod to $9 for an MP3 memory stick. Improvements in price are now so small they're hardly worth making.

Shipping an idea went from taking a month by boat to a few days by plane to overnight by Federal Express to a few minutes by fax to a moment by e-mail to instantaneous by Twitter. Now what? Will it arrive yesterday?

So, what's left is to make—to give—art. What's left is the generosity and humanity worth paying for. What's left is to take that resistance (the very same resistance we embraced and rewarded for decades) and destroy it.

Proof of the Resistance

It may be the resistance that's keeping you from embracing the ideas in this book. (Or it might be that I didn't make my case, but I'm betting on the former.) You're uncomfortable or skeptical or outright angry, but you're not sure why.

I mean, why not try art? How hard would it be to try?

You call the resistance "hard-hearted capitalist common sense." Perhaps you call it "being realistic about the system we live in." Better, I think, to call it stalling, a waste, and an insidious plot to keep you from doing your real work.

Don't let the lizard brain win.

Fear of Public Speaking

Why is it that a common, safe, and important task is so feared by so many people?

In *Iconoclast*, Gregory Berns uses his experience running a neuroscience research lab to explain the biological underpinnings of the resistance. In fact, public speaking is the perfect petri dish for exposing what makes us tick.

It turns out that the three biological factors that drive job performance and innovation are social intelligence, fear response, and perception. Public speaking brings all three together. Speaking to a group requires social intelligence. We need to be able to make an emotional connection with people, talk about what they are interested in, and persuade them. That's difficult, and we're not wired for this as well as we are wired to, say, eat fried foods.

Public speaking also triggers huge fear responses. We're surrounded by strangers or people of power, all of whom might harm us. Attention is focused on us, and attention (according to our biology) equals danger.

Last, and more subtly, speaking involves perception. It exposes how we see things, both the thing we are talking about and the response of the people in the room. Exposing that perception is frightening.

In a contest between the rational desire to spread an idea by giving a speech and the biological phobia against it, biology has an unfair advantage.

Where Is the Fear?

If there is no sale, look for the fear.

If a marketing meeting ends in a stalemate, look for the fear.

If someone has a tantrum, breaks a promise, or won't cooperate, there's fear involved.

Fear is the most important emotion we have. It kept our ancestors alive, after all. Fear dominates the other emotions, because without our ability to avoid death, the other ones don't matter very much.

Our sanitized, corporatized society hasn't figured out how to get rid of the fear, so instead we channel it into bizarre corners of our life. We check Twitter because of our fear of being left out. We buy expensive handbags for the same reason. We take a mundane follow-the-manual job because of our fear of failing as a map maker, and we make bad financial decisions because of our fear of taking responsibility for our money.

It turns out that we're even afraid to talk about fear, as if that somehow makes it more real.

Fear of living without a map is the main reason people are so insistent that we tell them what to do.

The reasons are pretty obvious: If it's someone else's map, it's not your fault if it doesn't work out. If you've memorized the sales script I gave you and you don't make the sale, who's in trouble now? Not only does the map insulate us from responsibility, but it's also a social talisman. We can tell our friends and family that we've found a good map, a safe map, a map worthy of respect.

Fear Self-fulfills

If the meeting you're about to call is the biggest, most important, do-or-die moment of your career, you're likely to feel some resistance and a lot of fear—which will not help the meeting go better. In fact, in negotiations, presentations, and other interactions, the smell of fear is the best indicator we have not to trust the other side.

The more you have to fear, the worse it goes.

One antidote is to pursue multiple paths, generating different ways to win. This meeting or that proposal no longer means everything. If nothing is do-or-die, then you don't have to worry so much about the dying part. Confidence self-fulfills as well. If you can bring more of it to an interaction, you're more likely to succeed, which of course creates more confidence for the next interaction. The cycle can bring you up, or it can bring you down. It's up to you.

If you're on a speaking tour with forty events booked, it doesn't seem as bad if one fails. If you have three great job opportunities, you can be a lot more comfortable in each interview. You may be saying, "Sure, that would be nice," but nice isn't the point. Effort gets you to this nice spot; effort and planning are tools to beat the resistance before it beats you.

The Paradox of the Safety Zone

The resistance would like you to curl up in a corner, avoid all threats, take no risks, and hide. It feels safe, after all.

The paradox is that the more you hide, the riskier it is. The less commotion you cause, the more likely you are to fail, to be ignored, to expose yourself to failure. We tried to set up an economy where you could hide your big ideas, go through the motions, and get what you needed. That's not working so well now.

The Resistance Works to Destroy the Tools That Oppose It

Getting Things Done could actually help you get things done. *A Whack on the Side of the Head* could help you be creative. Sales training could in fact help you make more sales. There are books and classes that can teach you how to do most of the things discussed in this book. And while many copies are sold and many classes attended, the failure rate is astonishingly high.

It's not because the books and classes aren't good. It's because the resistance is stronger.

Few people have the guts to point this out. Instead, we turn up our noses at the entire genre of self-help. We cynically ridicule the brown-nosers who set out to better themselves. We marginalize the teachers who are unaccredited or not affiliated with Harvard, et al. It's a brilliant plan by the resistance, and it usually works.

Don't listen to the cynics. They're cynics for a reason. For them, the resistance won a long time ago. When the resistance tells you not to listen to something, read something, or attend something, go. Do it. It's not an accident that successful people read more books.

Symptoms of the Lizard Brain

The resistance is everywhere, all the time. Its goal is to make you safe, which means invisible and unchanged. Visibility is dangerous. It leads to the possibility of people laughing at you, or even death. Change is dangerous because it involves moving from the known to the unknown, and that might be dangerous.

So, the resistance is wily. It works to do one of two things: get you to fit in (and become invisible) or get you to fail (which makes it unlikely that positive change will arrive, thus permitting you to stay still).

Here are some signs that the lizard brain is at work:

Don't ship on time. Late is the first step to never.

Procrastinate, claiming that you need to be perfect.

Ship early, sending out defective ideas, hoping they will be rejected.

Suffer anxiety about what to wear to an event.

Make excuses involving lack of money.

Do excessive networking with the goal of having everyone like you and support you.

Engage in deliberately provocative behavior designed to ostracize you so you'll have no standing in the community.

Demonstrate a lack of desire to obtain new skills.

Spend hours on obsessive data collection. (Jeffrey Eisenberg reports that "79 percent of businesses obsessively capture Internet traffic data, yet only 30 percent of them changed their sites as a result of analysis.")

Be snarky.

Start committees instead of taking action.

Join committees instead of leading.

Excessively criticize the work of your peers, thus unrealistically raising the bar for your work.

Produce deliberately outlandish work product that no one can possibly embrace.

Ship deliberately average work product that will certainly fit in and be ignored.

Don't ask questions.

Ask too many questions.

Criticize anyone who is doing something differently. If they succeed, that means you'll have to do something differently too.

Start a never-ending search for the next big thing, abandoning yesterday's thing as old.

Embrace an emotional attachment to the status quo.

Invent anxiety about the side effects of a new approach.

Be boring.

Focus on revenge or teaching someone a lesson, at the expense of doing the work.

Slow down as the deadline for completion approaches. Check your work obsessively as ship date looms.

Wait for tomorrow.

Manufacture anxiety about people stealing your ideas.

When you find behaviors that increase the chances of shipping, stop using them.

Believe it's about gifts and talents, not skill.

Announce you have neither.

This list is unusual in that I'm highlighting the up *and* the down, the left *and* the right. Any direction you go instead of the direction that succeeds is the work of the resistance.

It's interesting to say it out loud. "I'm doing this because of the resistance." "My lizard brain is making me anxious." "I'm angry right now because being angry is keeping me from doing my work."

When you say it out loud (not think it, but say it), the lizard brain retreats in shame.

"I Don't Know What to Do" and Other Classic Quotes from the Resistance

"I don't have any good ideas"—actually, you don't have any bad ideas. If you get enough bad ideas, the good ones will take care of themselves. And as every successful person will tell you, the ideas aren't the hard part. It's shipping that's difficult.

"I don't know what to do"—this one is certainly true. The question is, why does that bother you? No one actually knows what to do. Sometimes we have a hunch, or a good idea, but we're never sure. The art of challenging the resistance is doing something when you're not certain it's going to work.

"I didn't graduate from [insert brand of some prestigious educational institution here]"—well, MIT is now free online, for anyone who wants to learn. The public library in your town has just about everything you need, and what's not there is online. Access to knowledge used to matter. No longer.

"My boss won't let me"—of course she won't. Why would she? You're saying, "I want to do some crazy thing, and if it doesn't work, I want you to take all the blame. Of course, if it does work, I'll get the credit. Okay?" No, not okay. Nothing in this book argues that you need the perfect boss to become indispensable. I'm saying that if you become indispensable, you'll discover that you get a better boss.

"Well, that's fine for you, but my gender, race, health, religion, nationality, shoe size, handicap, or DNA don't make it easy"—Can't you just hear the lizard brain behind every word in this question? Precisely how many counterexamples do you need before you get over this excuse?

The Cult of Done

Bre Pettis wrote this manifesto on his blog:

1. There are three states of being. Not knowing, action and completion.
2. Accept that everything is a draft. It helps to get it done.

3. There is no editing stage.

4. Pretending you know what you're doing is almost the same as knowing what you are doing, so accept that you know what you're doing even if you don't and do it.

5. Banish procrastination. If you wait more than a week to get an idea done, abandon it.

6. The point of being done is not to finish but to get other things done.

7. Once you're done you can throw it away.

8. Laugh at perfection. It's boring and keeps you from being done.

9. People without dirty hands are wrong. Doing something makes you right.

10. Failure counts as done. So do mistakes.

11. Destruction is a variant of done.

12. If you have an idea and publish it on the Internet, that counts as a ghost of done.

13. Done is the engine of more.

The Work

Your real work, then, what you might be paid for, and what is certainly your passion, is simple: *the work*. The work is feeding and amplifying and glorifying the daemon.

Your work is to create art that changes things, to expose your insight and humanity in such a way that you are truly indispensable.

Your work is to do the work, not to do your job. Your job is about following instructions; the work is about making a difference. Your work is to ship. Ship things that make change.

Built to Ship

The habit that successful artists have developed is simple: they thrash a lot at the start, because starting means that they are going to finish. Not maybe, not probably, but going to.

If you want to produce things on time and on budget, all you have to do is work until you run out of time or run out of money. Then ship.

No room for stalling or excuses or the resistance. On ship date, it's gone.

Using Resistance as a Weather Vane

When you set out to do something that generates easy profits, indulges your temper, is selfish or shortsighted, it's unlikely you'll hear from the resistance. When the lizard brain is getting what it wants, it is definitely not going to slow you down.

You feel like yelling at your admin. Your conscience tells you not to, but you want to. The resistance is not a factor here. The voice telling you not to yell is your conscience, not your lizard brain.

You might feel the same feeling before you cheat on your taxes, go off your diet, or double-cross your partner. Listen to that feeling. It's not the resistance.

Every now and then you might hear from your conscience or you might hear your mom's voice in the back of your head, but you and I both know that this voice is different from the numbing paralysis of the resistance.

When you feel the resistance, the stall, the fear, and the pull, you know you're on to something. Whichever way the wind of resistance is coming from, that's the way to head—directly into the resistance. And the closer you get to achieving the breakthrough your genius has in mind, the stronger the wind will blow and the harder the resistance will fight to stop you.

I stopped writing this book a dozen times. Each time, the force that got me to pick it up again was the resistance. I realized that my lizard brain was afraid of this book, which is the best reason I can think of to write it.

Eating ice cream is easy. Making something that matters is hard. The resistance will help you find the thing you most *need* to do because it is the thing the resistance most wants to stop.

It's obvious. The resistance is afraid. The closer you come to unleashing the thing it fears, the harder it will fight.

Throwing Yourself Under the Bus

Actor John Goodman was interviewed about his role in *Waiting for Godot*. He had planned to spend the spring fishing and watching TV with his family in New Orleans, and he was prepared to turn the gig down. Here's his take on challenging the resistance:

"You're an idiot. This is a once-in-a-lifetime deal. It will never come by again . . . I didn't think I was up to it all. I had no confidence in myself. So it's just a matter of throwing myself under the bus and crawling my way out."

This posture of always challenging the resistance is what makes him a star.

"Right now, I'd rather be here than anywhere. I'd rather be here, trying to find the goddamn part, and I hope I never do find it, because I don't want to slide into complacency. What would I do then? Start cockfights in my dressing room?"

Steeper Near the Top

The closer you get to surfacing and then defeating the resistance, the harder it will fight you off.

If shipping were easy, you would have done it already.

Why the Lizard Brain Wants You to Be Stuck

In *The Dip*, I talk about how hard it is to quit a project (a job, a career, a relationship), even if the project is going absolutely nowhere.

It occurs to me that part of this pain comes from the resistance.

If it appears that you're fighting the good fight, laboring on, doing what you trained to do, then, hey, you're virtuous. You can proclaim victory without risk. There's not a lot to fear when you're stuck in the dip, not a lot that can threaten your standing. You're just a hardworking guy, doing your best; how dare someone criticize you?

The people who have experienced this and fought back—by quitting when they were stuck—tell me that the feeling of liberation and new potential is incredible. Suddenly, they can get back to doing the work, to making a difference, and to engaging with a community.

The hard part is distinguishing between quitting because the resistance wants you to (bad idea) or because the resistance doesn't want you to (great idea). The goal is to quit the tasks you're doing because you're hiding on behalf of the lizard brain and to push through the very tasks the lizard fears.

Is It Important Enough?

There really isn't a daemon, of course. There's only one "you," only one driver's license per person. You are going to invent what you're going to invent, do what you're going to do.

Van Gogh wasn't wired to paint. Paint was the medium available to him at the time. If he had lived today, perhaps he would have marketed organic tofu. It's not predetermined that you'll hold a paintbrush or write a symphony.

That means you have to choose your art. It's not preordained; there isn't only one art for you.

If you pick something that's beneath you, then the resistance will win. After all, what's the point of overcoming the pain the lizard brain inflicts if all you're doing is something that doesn't matter much anyway? Overcoming excuses and social challenges isn't easy, and it won't happen if the end result isn't worth it. Trivial art isn't worth the trouble it takes to produce it.

When you set down the path to create art, whatever sort of art it is, understand that the path is neither short nor easy. That means you must determine if the route is worth the effort. If it's not, dream bigger.

The Internet Is Crack Cocaine for the Resistance

If you sat at work all day watching *Hawaii Five-0* reruns, you'd probably lose your job. But it's apparently fine to tweak and update your Facebook account for an hour. That's "connecting to your social graph."

There's a big part of our psyche that wants to touch and be touched. We want to be connected, valued, and missed. We want people to know we exist and we don't want to get bored.

Waiting for the daemon can be boring or even frightening. So the resistance encourages us to flee, and where better to go than to the Internet? On a day when the resistance is in charge, I check my e-mail forty-five times. Why? Can't it wait? Of course it can, but it's fun. Fun to hear from people I like, fun to answer questions, fun to connect. If I had to be truthful, it's about resistance. E-mailing is fun, but it rarely changes the world.

Don't even get me started on Twitter. There are certainly people who are using it effectively and productively. Some people (a few) are finding that it helps them do the work. But the rest? It's perfect resistance, because it's never done. There's always another tweet to be read and responded to. Which, of course, keeps you from doing the work.

Where did your art go while you were tweeting?

Where Do You Hide Your Brilliance?

Where do you hide your insight? You have plenty of big ideas, no shortage of breakthroughs. A friend of mine says something really smart every day, something earth-shattering once a week. And that's it. At the end of the year, he has some great blog posts and a pile of Twitter tweets to show for it. What if he harnessed even one of those ideas and fought the resistance hard enough to actually make something of it?

At the end of the year, he could show us a multimillion-dollar company, or a movement that changed the world. By the end of the year, he could have leveraged a few of those ideas into a promotion, a corner office, a parking space.

The only difference between my friend and someone who changes everything is the resistance.

Tick Tick Tick

This is my twelfth book since 1999.

When I started my career, I was a book packager. My staff and I created more than a hundred titles, working with various publishers. After that, I started and sold an Internet company and then started a blog, gave some speeches, and started another Internet company.

Am I some sort of prodigy? I don't think so. I ship. I don't get in the way of the muse, I fight the resistance, and I ship. I do this by *not doing* an enormous number of tasks that are perfect stalling devices, ideal ways of introducing the resistance into our lives.

A workaholic brings fear into the equation. She works all the time to be sure everything is all right, and she experiences resistance all the time. She satisfies the raging fear of her lizard brain by being at the job site all the time, just to be sure.

I'm not a workaholic. There's no fear because I've ingrained the habit of shipping. The lizard brain has no chance, so it shuts up and finds something else to worry about.

By forcing myself to do absolutely no busywork tasks in between bouts with the work, I remove the best excuse the resistance has. I can't avoid the work because I am not distracting myself with anything *but* the work. This is the hallmark of a productive artist. I don't go to meetings. I don't write memos. I don't have a staff. I don't commute. The goal is to strip away anything that looks productive but doesn't involve shipping.

It takes crazy discipline to do nothing between projects. It means that you have to face a blank wall and you can't look busy. It means you are alone with your thoughts, and it means that a new project, perhaps a great project, will appear pretty soon, because your restless energy can't permit you to only sit and do nothing.

Leo Babauta's brilliant little book *Zen Habits* helps you think your way through this problem. His program is simple: Attempt to create only one significant work a year. Break that into smaller projects, and every day, find three tasks to accomplish that will help you complete a project. And do *only* that during your working hours. I'm talking about an hour a day to complete a mammoth work of art, whatever sort of art you have in mind. That hour a day might not be fun, but it's probably a lot more productive than the ten hours you spend now.

People sabotage Leo's idea every day. They try to do the significant project at the same time they pay lip service (and devote time) to all that surface nonsense that people say you're supposed to spend your time on. Since they try to do both, they accomplish neither. Or they pretend their project is significant, but it's actually trivial and far below them.

Letting silence into your day gives the daemon a chance to be heard from. The resistance is unable to proclaim that it's too busy tweeting, Facebooking, going to meetings, blogging, networking, paying bills, and traveling. No, actually, it's not busy at all. We're standing quietly, waiting to applaud our genius as he does his work.

The difference between a successful artist and a failed one happens *after* the idea is hatched. The difference is the race to completion. Did you finish?

Anxiety Is Practicing Failure in Advance

Anxiety is needless and imaginary. It's *fear about fear*, fear that means nothing.

The difference between fear and anxiety: Anxiety is diffuse and focuses on possibilities in an unknown future, not a real and present threat. The resistance is 100 percent about anxiety, because humans have developed other emotions and warnings to help us avoid actual threats. Anxiety, on the other hand, is an internal construct with no relation to the outside world. "Needless anxiety" is redundant, because anxiety is always needless. Anxiety doesn't protect you from danger, but from doing great things. It keeps you awake at night and foretells a future that's not going to happen.

On the other hand, fear is about staying alive, avoiding snakes, feeding your family, and getting the right to play again tomorrow. Fear should be paid careful attention. There's not a lot of genuine fear here in our world, so when it appears, it's worth noting.

Anxiety, on the other hand, is dangerous paralysis. Anxiety is the exaggeration of the worst possible what-if, accompanied by self-talk that leads to the relentless minimization of the actual odds of success.

Anxiety makes it impossible to do art, because it feeds the resistance, giving the lizard brain insane power over us. *It's impossible to be a linchpin if you agree to feed your anxiety.*

You'll notice that throughout this book I've often used the word "fear" when I really meant anxiety. That's because we do it all the time, confusing the two. A bad habit.

The Grateful Dread: Two Ways to Deal with Anxiety

You're lying in bed and you can't remember whether or not you left the kitchen light on. This quickly leads to all sorts of scenarios playing on your internal movie screen, including midnight robberies, home invasions, and more. Like most episodes of anxiety, there are two responses. I'd like to argue that the first puts you on an endless treadmill, while the second (much more difficult) approach leads to all sorts of good outcomes.

The first approach is to seek reassurance. Get out of bed and check the light. After all, there are burglars in the bushes just waiting for you to fall asleep without that light on—checking to be sure it's on is the best way to get them to run away and find another house. This approach says that if you're worried about something, indulge the worry by asking people to *prove* that everything is going to be okay. Check in constantly, measure and repeat. "Is everything okay?" Reward the anxiety with reassurance and positive feedback. Of course, this just leads to more anxiety, because everyone likes reassurance and positive feedback. After you check the light, you might want to check the window locks and then recheck the light, just to be sure.

The second approach is to sit with the anxiety, don't run from it. Acknowledge it, explore it, befriend it. It's there, you're used to it, move on. *No rewards for worriers.* No water to put out this particular fire.

The problem with reassurance is that it creates a cycle that never ends. Reassure me about one issue and you can bet I'll find something else to worry about. Reassurance doesn't address the issue of anxiety; in fact, it exacerbates it. You have an itch and you scratch it. The itch is a bother, the scratch feels good, and so you repeat it forever, until you are bleeding.

The idea of sitting with your anxiety appears to be ludicrous, at least at first. To sit with something so uncomfortable isn't natural. The more you sit, the worse it gets. Without water, the fire rages. Throughout, you remain placid. The anxiety is there, it's real, but you merely acknowledge it, you don't flatter it with rationalization or even adrenaline. It just is, and you embrace it, like a hot day at the beach (or a cold day in Minnesota).

Then, an interesting thing happens. It burns itself out. The anxiety can't sustain itself forever, especially when morning comes and your house hasn't been invaded, when the speech is over and you haven't been laughed at, when the review is complete and you haven't been fired. Reality is the best reassurance of all. Over time, the cycle is broken. The resistance knows that the anxiety trick doesn't work anymore, especially if you're friendly to the anxiety. Pretty quickly, the anxiety cycles start to diminish and eventually peter themselves out.

Don't ask me to tell you that everything is going to be all right. I have no idea, for starters. And my palliative opinion actually will make your anxiety worse in the long run.

Anxiety and *Shenpa*

Shenpa is a Tibetan word that roughly means "scratching the itch." I think of it as a spiral of pain, something that is triggered by a small event and immediately takes you totally off the ranch. A small itch gets scratched, which makes it itch more, so you scratch more and more until you're literally in pain.

A police car appears in your rearview mirror. Perhaps you were going five miles an hour too fast. For many people, getting pulled over is a hassle, but no big deal. For someone with anxiety about this particular interaction, the mind races. The cop will harass you, you will fight back, it will escalate, you'll be arrested, they'll frame you for something else, and you'll end up in jail for the rest of your life! No wonder you're stressed when you finally pull over. You've been so busy eating prison food that there's not even time to breathe.

Your boss criticizes you at work. Not a big issue, just a gentle criticism. But your *shenpa* is a reflex that forces you to answer every criticism with a defense and a criticism in return. Unfortunately for you, your boss feels the same way. He's annoyed that you couldn't accept his feedback, and now the two of you are caught in a nasty cycle, one that won't end well.

You're on a sales call and it seems to be going well. This is your particular trigger. It might lead to a sale and that would expose you to all sorts of danger, says the lizard. So you say something stupid as a defense mechanism, which leads to a stumble in the rhythm of the meeting. You say something else stupid and suddenly, as you expected, it all begins to unravel. This is your *shenpa*, the one you invented for yourself.

The lizard brain is responsible for *shenpa*. It's the interaction between our normal rational world and the intense fears that the lizard lives with every day. Fortunately, we don't have our *shenpa* with everything. There are only a few things that can get any of us spinning out of control.

The best time to stop the spiral is the very first moment. Taking action at the start, calling it out, recognizing the cycle—this is your first and best chance. Embrace the itch from the start, but don't scratch it. To do otherwise is to lose all perspective. You can't make a useful map when you're busy exaggerating the downside of every option. This is *prajna*. If you can't teach the world a lesson, accept it, don't get attached to a different outcome.

"Sorry, Officer," you say, forcing yourself to sit quietly. And then he drives away.

Why didn't you end up in jail? Because you didn't scratch the itch. Because you didn't project fear and anxiety and anger, the cop didn't react with the same. You sat with the anxiety; you didn't run from it or bargain with it. You stayed.

"Thanks for the feedback, boss," you say. Then you repeat the feedback in your own words, to confirm to him that you heard him, and you walk away. It only took you three seconds, and you avoided an hour of pain.

Why didn't the entire day get ruined? Because you didn't scratch the itch. You were aware enough of the boss's posture and his *shenpa* that you didn't continue the cycle.

Shenpa and Social Connection

For many people, *shenpa* and anxiety are related to community. Whether it's throwing a party, joining a club, attending a meeting, or giving a speech, it tends to involve interactions with other people.

The killer: our anxiety not only makes us miserable, but ruins the interaction. People smell it on you. They react to it. They're less likely to hire you or buy from you or have fun at your party. The very thing you are afraid of occurs, precisely because you are afraid of it, which of course makes the *shenpa* cycle even worse.

Shenpa is caused by a conflict between the lizard brain (which wants to strike out or to flee) and the rest of our brain, which desires achievement, connection, and grace. Oscillating between the two merely makes things worse. It seems that you have two choices for ending the cycle: you can flee or you can stay.

There's nothing inherently wrong with fleeing. If you can't handle a certain kind of interaction or event, don't do it. Avoid it. Some people weren't born to be baseball umpires.

The other alternative is to stay. If you believe that it's important enough, then your challenge is to overrule the resistance. Not to flee and return, flee and return. No, you must stay. Sit with it. Give the resistance no quarter. Just stay.

During a sales call, in that moment when you would break the silence to give the squirming lizard some solace, don't. Sit. Wait the prospect out. The more you want to give in to the inner voice of anxiety, the more resilient you become. Waiting isn't easy, which is precisely why it is so effective when engaging with other people. The quiet strength it takes to withstand the urge to flee builds confidence in those around you.

I was in a high-stakes negotiation last week. The resistance was screaming at me to fold, to fight back, to surrender, to do anything. Just make it stop! Make it okay!

I heard the lizard and did nothing. I sat with the squirming, sat with the itch, just sat.

The result was a wave of confidence, because finally, after watching me sit for two days without panic, the lizard realized I wasn't going to change my position. It quieted down. I was back in charge of myself. The result was freedom. I was free to be calm and generous and clear in the negotiation, and it turned out far better than I had hoped. If the resistance had been in charge, the entire project would have crashed and burned.

P.S.: Never let the lizard send an e-mail.

"People Will Laugh at Me"

This is the heart of the matter.

There certainly used to be important evolutionary reasons to avoid risk. Saber-tooth tigers, for example, could really ruin your day.

Now, however, for almost all the art I'm talking about, the only risk is the loss of some time (time you were wasting anyway) and the very real chance that people will laugh at you.

High school.

It often seems to come down to high school.

As you wrestle with the resistance and you make a list of all the reasons you're skeptical, overly busy, cash-poor, and generally unable to do some art, please add to the list "and people will laugh at me if I try."

Good. Now at least you have one genuine reason on the list.

Have people ever laughed at you? Not with you, but at you? Derisively. With relish. We remember that all our lives, and it's affecting the decisions you make today, even though the people who laughed at you in school don't even remember your name.

(*Shenpa* and Turbulence)

My friend Jon likes it when an airplane hits heavy turbulence. His insight is worth sharing. "The odds of a plane crashing from turbulence are essentially zero, so I sit and enjoy it. It's like a ride at an amusement park."

I'm writing this as my plane hits heavy turbulence and it turns out that he's right. The moment I stopped trying to will the plane to stay in the air and started enjoying the ride, it got a lot more fun, and it turns out that the pilot didn't need my help in keeping the plane aloft.

Shenpa and Income and Success

In the factory age, *shenpa* was a pain in the neck—it made you neurotic and no fun to be around. But you could still have a decent job and still be successful, because your neuroses were on your own time. Your job on the assembly line was too banal to cause the cycle of *shenpa*. Instead, you did that at home.

Now, though, in a world where linchpins are valued and cogs are not, it seems as though unchecked anxiety is the single biggest barrier between you and your goals. Given the choice, people don't hire or work with or trust or follow people who get stuck in a cycle of anxiety. You're toxic and we don't want to spend all our time reassuring you. Worse, if you live in a state of anxiety about tasks that are in demand (like art, brave action, and generosity), it's going to change what you choose to do. You'll avoid the very things that would make you indispensable.

I don't want to be around people who are in frequent cycles of pain and fear.

Suddenly, *shenpa* affects your pocketbook as much as your psyche.

Watching the Watching

My favorite pastime when traveling is watching people watching.

Susan (not her real name) is waiting for someone at a hotel in Chicago (not the actual city). She's well dressed, with sunglasses on her blond (not her real color) hair. Here's her cycle, which she repeats every sixteen seconds (I timed it):

> She looks left, then right.
>
> Adjusts the hair over her left ear.

Looks ahead to see if anyone is watching.

Adjusts her sunglasses.

Pulls her skirt down a quarter of an inch.

Adjusts the hair over her right ear.

Repeat.

Over and over and over. This is obviously not intentional behavior; it's baked in. Her ancestors did it on the savanna, and she's doing it here. It matters a great deal what the herd thinks of her. Instead of creating something, connecting, or learning, she's stuck in a lizard cycle of preening and fear.

When the resistance settles in, here's the cycle my lizard brain forces me into:

Check my e-mail box to see what people think of my work. Answer them.

Check the tribes online site to see what's going on. Adjust if necessary.

Check my e-mail box.

Check my blog feeds to see what's happening. Read the relevant ones; comment if appropriate.

Check the status of my Squidoo pages.

Repeat.

I can do this forever. It's like adjusting a pair of sunglasses. It never ends.

Artists never do this while they're being artists. When I put myself on an Internet diet (only five checks a day, not fifty), my productivity tripled. Tripled.

Sprint!

The best way to overcome your fear of creativity, brainstorming, intelligent risk-taking, or navigating a tricky situation might be to sprint.

When we sprint, all the internal dialogue falls away and we focus on going as fast as we possibly can. When you're sprinting, you don't feel that sore knee and you don't worry that the ground isn't perfectly level. You just run.

You can't sprint forever. That's what makes it sprinting. The brevity of the event is a key part of why it works.

"Quick, you have thirty minutes to come up with ten business ideas."

"Hurry, we need to write a new script for our commercial . . . we have fifteen minutes."

My first huge project was launching a major brand of science-fiction computer adventure games (Ray Bradbury, Michael Crichton, etc.). I stopped going to business school classes in order to do the launch.

One day, right after a red-eye flight, the president of the company told me that he had canceled the project. He said that the company didn't have enough resources to launch all the products we had planned, our progress was too slow, and the packaging wasn't ready yet.

I went to my office and spent the next twenty hours rewriting every word of text, redesigning every package, rebuilding every schedule, and inventing a new promotional strategy. It was probably six weeks of work for a motivated committee, and I did it (alone) in one swoop. Like lifting a car off an infant, it was impossible, and I have no recollection at all of the project now.

The board saw the finished work, reconsidered, and the project was back on again. I didn't get scared until after the sprint (then I passed out). You can't sprint every day, but it's probably a good idea to sprint regularly. It keeps the resistance at bay.

Downhill Versus Uphill

Launching your art into the world often feels like an uphill climb, an ongoing series of challenges and obstacles. At any step along the way, the resistance can cut you down. All you need to do is falter, and your work is wasted. You're pushing a rock uphill, and if you stop for a second, the thing rolls all the way down, erasing all your effort.

It's possible, though, to view the work that comes with the launching of your art as an inevitable gravitational process, like an avalanche or a giant slalom. Start at the top of the hill, not the bottom. One little step to get you started, and then it grows and grows, ever faster. No amount of resistance can stop this from happening.

The Internet can amplify this effect. You put up a video, and then in a week, a million people have seen it. You send an e-mail message to the right six people, and a project begins.

That's why authors enjoy having book publishers. Even though it's technically easy to publish your own book, technically easy to get it typeset or printed or even put into a bookstore, authors with a choice rarely self-publish. That's because the current system is such a powerful amplifier. Send your manuscript to your agent. She sells it to a publisher (no pushing necessary on your behalf). The publisher does all the difficult tasks of bringing your work to market, tasks that your lizard brain would gladly sabotage.

If there's an infrastructure (like a publisher) in place to amplify your insights, that's great. Often, though, it's not there. The firms that take money to patent your idea and promote it, say, or the fraudulent contests that charge you money to enter a competition to win a prize—these prey on people who haven't built a platform. You need a platform that makes it easy to turn your insight into a movement.

I'm trying to sell you on the idea of building a platform *before* you have your next idea, to view the platform building as a separate project from spreading your art. You can work on the platform every day, do it without facing the resistance. As the platform gets bigger and stronger, you get to launch each idea a little farther uphill.

It's not easy to get to this point. A valuable platform is an asset, one that isn't handed to you. It takes preparation and effort to set the world up so that your ideas are more likely to ship. But that's effort that the resistance won't be so eager to sabotage. By separating the hard work of preparation from the scary work of insight, you can build an environment in which you're more likely to ship.

One Way to Thrash and Overcome Resistance

Here's how I make stuff.

I've used this technique to launch multimillion-dollar software projects, write books, plan vacations, work in teams, work solo, and write a blog. All projects that ship on time.

The first step is write down the due date. Post it on the wall. It's real. You will ship on this date, done or not.

The next step is to use index cards, Post-it notes, Moleskine notebooks, fortune cookies, whatever you can embrace. Write down every single notion, plan, idea, sketch, and contact. This is when you go fishing. Get as much help as you like. Invite as many people in as you can. This is their big chance.

This is where the thrashing and dreaming begin. It's very hard to get the people you work with to pay attention at this moment. Since the deadline is so far away, their lizard brains are asleep and there's no fear or selfish motivation available. People focus on emergencies, not urgencies, and getting yourself (and them) to stop working on tomorrow's deadline and pitch in now isn't easy. A big part of the work, then, is to get yourself (and your team, if you have one) to step up and dream.

On a regular basis, collate the cards and read 'em aloud to the team. This process will inevitably lead to more cards.

Then, put the cards into a database. I use FileMaker Pro, but you can use any simple database. (You can even use a pad of paper.) If you have a group, try to find a group database for the Web. Every card gets its own record.

The record can include words, images, sketches, and links to other cards. The idea is that this is your thrashing playground. Let the team play along. Rearrange. Draw. Sketch. Make sure everyone understands that this is *the very last chance they have to make the project better.*

One person (that would be you) then goes through the database and builds a complete description of the project. If it's a book, then you've got a forty-page outline. If it's a Web site, then you have every single screen and feature. If it's a conference, then you have an agenda, a menu, a list of venues, and so on. It's the blueprint.

Take this blueprint NOT to everyone, but to the few people who have sign-off control, the people with money, your boss. They can approve it, cancel the project, or suggest a few compromises.

Then say, "If I deliver what you approved, on budget and on time, will you ship it?"

Don't proceed until you get a yes. Iterate if you must, but don't get started simply because you're in a hurry. Do not accept "Well, I'll know it when I see it." Not allowed.

Once you get your yes, go away and build your project, thrash-free. Ship on time, because that's what a linchpin does.

Rethinking Your Goals in Light of the Resistance

What does the success of your project look like? Have you defined success in terms of critics, or some other measure that doesn't actually serve your needs? Are you hoping for a great review or a gold star or applause? A profit? Big sales? Changing people's minds? The chance to do it again?

The resistance is happy to set up unachievable goals as a way of dissuading you from doing the work. After all, if it's impossible to achieve something and it's going to be painful to try, why bother? When we agree to define our success on others' terms, especially other people who don't particularly like us and aren't inclined to root for us, we're giving in to the resistance.

If you decide you want to please the critics, the same people who make a living hating the sort of thing you do, it's easy to give up in advance.

If you declare that you want to build a giant brand, something in the top fifty of all brands of all time, it's easy to hit roadblocks. That's because your goal is largely impossible. The roadblocks don't make your project more likely to succeed; they kill it.

The Grateful Dead puzzled industry pundits for a long time. Why didn't they want to sell more records? Why didn't they want a gold record? Why didn't they want to get their music played on the radio? The answer is simple: they were playing a different game, a different tune. Instead of buying into a system that would tear them down and corrupt their vision, they built their own system, one that was largely resistance-proof. One concert a night, night after night, for decade after decade. Play only for people you like, with people you enjoy. How can the lizard brain object to that?

The result is sneaky and effective. When you haven't set up a judge and jury for your work, you get to do art that doesn't alert the resistance. And then you can leverage that art into the next thing.

Amplifying Little Thoughts

Do you remember what you had for lunch yesterday? If you take a second, you probably do. Now, do you remember what internal dialogue and little thoughts you had racing through your mind a few minutes before lunch yesterday? Almost certainly not.

Little thoughts are ephemeral. They come, and inevitably, they go. We don't remember them an hour later, never mind a week or a month later.

A decade ago, I came up with the idea for *Permission Marketing*. In the shower. I still remember the where and the when. It was one of those little ideas, something that could easily disappear. The resistance would be happy if all your little brainstorms disappeared, because then they wouldn't represent a threat, would they?

The challenge is in being alert enough to write them down, to prioritize them, to build them, and to ship them out the door. It's a habit, it's easy to learn, and it's frightening.

The Resistance Gets Its Next Excuse Ready in Advance

Are you in the wrong industry? Does your spouse hold you back? Is it the economy? Perhaps it's the vendetta your boss has always had against you.

The resistance is working overtime to be sure that you won't actually do anything remarkable. As a result, the list of excuses in reserve is longer than you might expect. When it finds a useful crutch, a loser's limp, the resistance will milk it for all it's worth. But removing that excuse, calling the bluff, probably won't be sufficient. There's always another one at the ready.

The only solution is to call all the bluffs at once, to tolerate no rational or irrational reason to hold back on your art. The only solution is to start today, to start now, and to ship.

THE POWERFUL
CULTURE OF GIFTS

Gifts?

I must have been absent that day at Stanford business school.

They don't spend a lot of time teaching you about the power of unreciprocated gifts, about the long (fifty thousand years) tradition of tribal economies being built around the idea of mutual support and generosity. In fact, I don't think the concept is even mentioned once. We've been so brainwashed, it doesn't even occur to us that there might be an alternative to "How much should I charge, how much can I make?"

There are three reasons why it's now urgent to understand how gift culture works. First, the Internet (and digital goods) has lowered the marginal cost of generosity. Second, it's impossible to be an artist without understanding the power that giving a gift creates. And third, the dynamic of gift giving can diminish the cries of the resistance and permit you to do your best work.

The very fact that gift giving without recompense feels uncomfortable is reason enough for you to take a moment to find out why.

Giving, Receiving, Giving

In the beginning, there was the culture of potlatch and gifts. Caveman culture has a long tradition of reciprocity, and as Marcel Mauss has written, this reciprocity was used to build relationships and power. In the Pacific Northwest, Native American tribe leaders established their power by giving *everything* away. They could afford to give everyone a gift, because they were so powerful and the gifts were a symbol of that power. Any leader who hoarded saw his power quickly diminish. Mauss argued that there is no such thing as a free gift. Everyone who gives a gift, he asserts, wants something in return.

Then, quite suddenly, this ancient tradition changed. Money and structured society flipped the system, and now you get, you don't give. Author Lewis Hyde reminds us that for the last few centuries, our society has said that the winner was the person who *received* the most gifts. To receive a gift made you a king, a rich person, someone worth currying favor with. It feels totally appropriate that people in power are pandered to. It turns out, though, that this is a fairly recent behavior. Power used to be about giving, not getting.

In the linchpin economy, the winners are once again the artists who *give* gifts. Giving a gift makes you indispensable. Inventing a gift, creating art—that is what the market seeks out, and the givers are the ones who earn our respect and attention. Shepard Fairey didn't seek to monetize the Obama Hope poster. He gave it away with a single-minded obsession. The more copies he gave away, the closer he came to achieving his political, personal, and professional goals.

Part of the reason for this flip is the digital nature of our new gift system. If I create an idea, the Internet makes it possible for that gift to spread everywhere, quite quickly, at no cost to me. Digital gifts, ideas that spread—these allow the artist to be far more generous than he could ever be in an analog world.

Thomas Hawk is the most successful digital photographer in the world. He has taken tens of thousands of pictures, on his way to his goal of taking a million in his lifetime. The remarkable thing about Hawk's rise is that his pictures are licensed under the Creative Commons license and are freely shared with anyone, with no permission required for personal use. Thomas is both an artist and a giver of gifts. The result is that he leads a tribe, he has plenty of paid work, and he is known for his talents. In short, he is indispensable.

When users of the online review site Yelp ganged up on a pizze-ria in San Francisco, management didn't sue. Instead, they got creative and gave generously. Pizzeria Delfina outfitted its servers with T-shirts emblazoned with the most ridiculous one-star criticisms the place had received. The idea spread, and the T-shirts have shown up online around the world. They cost next to nothing, but millions got a smile. Delfina gave a gift to its loyal customers by making fun of itself.

We Can Never Repay Keller Williams

Keller Williams is a maestro, a genius, and a guitarist for a new era.

Using digital loops, he performs on eight guitars at the same time. Barefoot on stage, he mixes the sounds, carefully setting a guitar on the floor and walking over to a mixing board to bring up one sound or another, all live, with no prerecording or gimmicks.

His concert is a gift. There's no way any one person in the audi-ence can repay Keller. The ticket sales and the applause pale in com-parison to the preparation, effort, and sheer genius Keller puts into each performance.

And online, his music is free—free to download, free to share.

The fact that we can't repay him is precisely why his gift is so valuable, and why so many people are eager to pay for the privilege of being in the room with him. Keller builds a tribe by giving, not by taking.

As I wrote in my previous book, *Tribes*, the new form of marketing is leadership, and leadership is about building and connecting tribes of like-minded people. Keller's generosity to his tribe doesn't only connect him to them; it connects the tribe members to one another. One fan is automatically the friend of the next, if for no other reason than to share the effects of Williams's generosity.

Capitalism has taught us that every transaction has to be fair, an even trade for goods or services delivered. What Keller and other artists demonstrate is that linchpin thinking is about delivering gifts that can never be adequately paid for.

There Are No Artists on the Assembly Line

As soon as it is part of a system, it's not art.

Artists shake things up. They invent as they go; they respond to inputs and create surprising new outputs. That's why MBAs often have trouble pigeonholing artists. Artists can't be easily instructed, predicted, or measured, and that's precisely what you are taught to do in business school.

Consumers love artists. So do investors. That's because art represents a chance to improve the status quo, not just make it cheaper. Art builds a community, and the community creates value for all.

When U2 goes on tour, the tour is an opportunity to do new art every night. The moment the band turns the tour into a cookie-cutter system to earn money, it ceases to be art and becomes a souvenir factory.

There are services online that will take your photograph and turn it into an Andy Warhol–style silkscreen. While this might be artistic, it's not art. Any time you can say "xxx-style," it has ceased to be art and started to be a process.

Selfish

Robert Ringer wrote *Looking Out for Number One*, one of the most damaging business books I've ever read. His salute to selfishness was a product of its time, and it rubbed a lot of people the wrong way.

Becoming a linchpin is not an act of selfishness. I see it as an act of generosity, because it gives you a platform for expending emotional labor and giving gifts. There are plenty of bosses who fear the idea of indispensable employees and would instead encourage you to focus on teamwork. "Teamwork" is the word bosses and coaches and teachers use when they actually mean, "Do what I say." It's not teamwork to stand by and do whatever the captain or the supervisor tells you to. It might be cooperative or compliant or useful, but it's not teamwork.

The only way I know of to become a successful linchpin is to build a support team of fellow linchpins. The goal is to have an impact, and while it starts with the person (this is my gift, my effort), it works only when it is gratefully accepted by your team and your customers.

The Curse of Reciprocity

It's human nature. If someone gives you a gift, you need to reciprocate.

If someone invites you over for dinner, you bring cookies. If people give you a Christmas gift, you can't rest until you give them one back.

It's reciprocity that turned the gift system into the gift economy. Suddenly, giving a gift becomes an obligation, one demanding payment, not a gift at all. So marketers use the reciprocity impulse against us, using gifts as a come-on.

This can cripple your art.

You best give a gift without knowing or being concerned with whether it will be repaid. A waiter does his art for table twelve regardless of whether or not those customers are big tippers. An artist paints his painting without knowing if someone is going to buy it.

The magic of the gift system is that the gift is voluntary, not part of a contract. The gift binds the recipient to the giver, and both of them to the community. A contract *isolates* individuals, with money as the connector. The gift binds them instead.

Gifts as a Signal of Surplus

It's difficult to be generous when you're hungry.

Yet being generous keeps you from going hungry. Hence the conflict.

A business coach writes and gives away a two-hundred-page e-book jammed with useful tips and secrets. Everything he knows, online, for free. Is this generous or stupid? Is there an easier way to make it clear that he has wisdom to spare?

Gifts not only satisfy our needs as artists, they also signal to the world that we have plenty more to share. This perspective is magnetic. The more you have in your cup, the more likely people are to want a drink.

If I meet you at a party, I hope you'll ask me for free marketing advice.

I'm always amazed that people are willing to listen to what I have to say and I'm happy to share. The act of giving the gift is worth more to me than it may be to you to receive.

(Dunbar's Number and the Small World)

British anthropologist Robin Dunbar theorized that a typical person can't easily have more than 150 people in his tribe. After 150 friends and fellow citizens, we can't keep track. It's too complicated.

For tens of thousands of years, our nomadic ways, small villages, and lack of transport kept the world small. The key unit of tribal measure was the village or the nomadic tribe. When our community got too big, it split and people moved on—we needed to know the people in our tribe, and since we couldn't process more than a hundred and fifty people, we divided. We had a brotherhood, an extended family, people who watched our back, helped us succeed, and did business with us.

When we meet a stranger, we do business. When we encounter a member of the tribe, we give gifts.

Technology (travel, communication, and manufactured goods) meant that a few thousand years ago, a great leap of productivity was ready to occur. This leap could occur only if we had more people to trade with, more people to hire and interact with. We could make the leap if we were able to make the world bigger. This need to make the world bigger, though, conflicted with our cultural and biological desire to keep the world small.

A lot of the stress we feel in the modern world comes from this conflict between the small world in which we're wired to exist and the large world we use to make a living.

Gifts Make the Tribe

The biblical proscription against usury goes all the way back to Moses. The rule was simple: you couldn't charge interest on a loan to anyone in your tribe. Strangers, on the other hand, paid interest. This isn't a matter of ancient biblical archeology; the edict against interest stuck for thousands of years, until around the time of Columbus.

It's worth taking a minute to understand the reasoning here.

If money circulates freely within the tribe, the tribe will grow prosperous more quickly. I give you some money to buy seeds, your farm flourishes, and now we both have money to give to someone else to invest. The faster the money circulates, the better the tribe does. The alternative is a tribe of hoarders, with most people struggling to find enough resources to improve productivity.

Obviously, there's another force at work here. When I make an interest-free loan to you, I'm trusting you and giving you a gift at the same time. This interaction increases the quality of our bond and strengthens the community. Just as you wouldn't charge your husband interest on a loan, you don't charge a tribe member.

Strangers, on the other hand, are not to be trusted. Going further, strangers don't deserve the bond that the gift brings. It would turn the stranger into a tribe member, and the tribe is already too big. If I loan money to a stranger, I'm doing it for one reason: to make money. I risk my money, and if all goes well, we both profit. But there's no bond here, no connection.

One reason that art has so much power is that it represents the most precious gift we can deliver. And delivering it to people we work with or connect with strengthens our bond with them. It strengthens the tribal connection.

When you walk into your boss's office and ask for advice, she doesn't charge you an hourly fee, even if she's a corporate coach or a psychoanalyst, even if you want help with a personal problem. The gift of her time and attention and insight is just that—a gift. As a result, the bond between you strengthens.

(Martin Luther and the Beginning of the Money Culture)

The Protestant Reformation permitted the explosion of commerce that led to the world we live in now. Once the Reformation began to spread, Martin Luther was heavily lobbied by powerful local interests. In response, he gave princes and landlords the moral authority to take over the commons and rent the land back to the people who lived on it.

The new church was looking for political support, and its embrace of mercantilism guaranteed that it would get that support from power brokers that had chafed under the Catholic Church's opposition to the practice of charging interest and the commercialization of formerly common lands. (The Catholic Church wanted to keep local lords, princes, and kings weak, of course, because it was built around a strong universal leader, the pope.)

One of the factors in the growth of the Protestant Reformation was that commercial interests supported its spread because they needed the moral authority to lend and borrow money. It's hard to overestimate how large of a shift this led to in the world's culture and economics.

As Thomas Jefferson wrote, it created a world where "the merchant has no homeland." If everyone is a stranger, it's a lot easier to do business. If everyone is a stranger, then we can charge for things that used to be gifts. The merchant class was essential to imperialism and to the growth of the money culture, but it can't exist without a culture that encourages moneylending.

This thinking destroyed many traditional tribes, but permitted the growth of commerce-based organizations. The East India Company or the fashion houses of France or the banks of Italy could never have existed in a world that honored a ban on usury.

Martin Luther saw that embracing the needs of local power brokers could enhance the spread of Protestantism. With little alternative, the pope followed suit. The ban on usury was refined, double-talked, and eventually eliminated. The money flowed, investments were made, businesses grew, and productivity soared. People could view every transaction as a chance to lend or make money because they were independent agents. Everyone became a businessman, a borrower, or a lender.

Suddenly, your tribe was a profit center. If you knew a lot of people, you could make money from them. Social leadership magically translated into financial leadership.

For the last five hundred years, the best way to succeed has been to treat everyone as a stranger you could do business with. This is one reason that some multilevel marketers and insurance salesmen make people nervous. It seems to cross the tiny remaining gulf between business and the tribe. As the lines have crossed, we've abandoned the idea of a village as a tribe. Instead, we're left with the tribe of our birth family and the tribe at work. We practically live with the people we work with, and we identify with them.

Now we live in a world where corporate tribe members are likely to be as important to us as family. Do you talk to your sister more often than you talk to your boss? What about the head of Midwest sales?

Human beings have a need for a tribe, but the makeup of that tribe has changed, probably forever. Now, the tribe is composed of our coworkers or our best customers, not only our family or our village or religious group.

This double shift means that the best professional entanglements aren't with strangers; they are with the tribe. Given a choice between an insider or an outsider, we choose to work with insiders. But tribe members are family, and we shouldn't be charging them interest! Tighter bonds produce better results, and so the gift culture returns. Full circle, from gift to usury and back to gift.

A loan without interest is a gift. A gift brings tribe members closer together. A gift can make you indispensable.

The Forgotten Act of the Gift

For five hundred years, since the legalization of usury and the institutionalization of money, almost every element of our lives has been about commerce.

If you did something, you did it for money, or because it would lead to money. Sure, you still don't charge your kids for dinner, but you also don't encourage your kids to sweep up at the supermarket for free. Why should they? It's someone's *job*.

Example: I'm going downtown by cab from the airport. There are forty fellow travelers in the cab line. If I call out, "Anyone want to share a cab to the Marriott?" people look at me funny. They don't want to owe me for the ride, don't want to interact, don't want to open themselves up to the connection that will occur from taking my gift of a ride. They'd rather pay for it, clean and square, and stay isolated. It's hard to imagine two Bedouin tribespeople isolating from each other with such enthusiasm.

Gifts have been relegated to cash substitutes. If I give you a gift, the only apparent reason is to get you to reciprocate. It's like giving you cash, but with social cover. The studio chief thinks, "I can give Seth Rogen a pinball machine for Christmas, because then he'll owe me and the next negotiation might go better."

The first problem, of course, with these sorts of gifts is that it ruins true gifts, while the second problem is that they are poor cash substitutes. They create misunderstandings and confusion because if Seth Rogen doesn't value the pinball machine the way the studio head does, one side or the other is going to be upset.

Real gifts don't demand reciprocation (at least not direct reciprocation), and the best kinds of gifts are gifts of art.

Alcoholics Anonymous and Gifts

A critical underpinning at AA is that no money changes hands. There's no central organization collecting dues, no fee to attend a meeting, no payments from one member to another. The act of helping a fellow alcoholic for free has two effects: First, it brings the giver and the recipient closer together, creating a tribe. And second, it creates an obligation for the recipient. Not an obligation to reciprocate, because she really can't and it's not expected, but an obligation to help the next person.

And so the movement grows.

The Difference Between Debt and Equity

When someone invests in your business and takes some founder's stock, he gets closer to you. He is on your side, because when you win, he wins.

When a bank loans you money for college, it becomes the Other. The bank is opposed to you, sapping your resources and taking money first, not last. College loans are the ones you can't discharge, even in bankruptcy. The bank that made the loan usually sells it, so there's no connection to you any longer. The bank doesn't offer counseling or peer support or even check in with you about your career choices. They just demand to be paid. No equity investor would act this way.

There are many forms of equity, and few of them involve cash. When you invest time or resources into someone's success or happiness, and your payment is a share of that outcome, you become partners.

What Does All This Have to Do with You?

Are you giving gifts? Really and truly? Or are you so beaten down by the system, so indoctrinated by it that you can't imagine creating art and getting closer to the people who matter to you?

If this section on gifts and debt and reciprocity feels strange, it's a symptom of how much humanity has been drummed out of you by a commercial imperative run amok—or possibly it's a symptom that you've forgotten that you even have the ability to give these gifts. The system makes you feel taken advantage of, abused, exploited by the "commercial imperative." You're just a player in the commercial machine. Realizing you haven't given gifts because you're scared or that you've forgotten what you have to offer might compel you to action.

I think it's worth a try.

The Circles of the Gift System

While some artists get rich (J. K. Rowling got very rich), making art is not about getting rich. Art is a gift, a gift from the artist to the viewer, the listener, the user. The moment it ceases to be a gift, some of the art is lost.

A change has happened to the working life of a typical artist. Now, your art can reach much further and affect more people than ever before. A folksinger can reach a million people with her gift, not just a coffeehouse full. An industrial designer can impact the lives of a billion people with a new way to filter water.

Many people have fretted about the economics of this cost-free spread of art in all its forms, but the real magic is the leverage this expansion adds, not the loss of commerce it causes. When you have more friends in the core circle, more people with whom to share your art, your art is amplified and can have more power.

Remember, we're most likely to give gifts to our family and friends. We don't charge them interest, and they are not customers; they are people we embrace.

The Internet is changing the circle we call "family and friends." Twitter and Facebook created a new class of people; call them "friendlies." If I can give the gift of art, for free, to my expanding circle of friendlies, why would I hesitate?

Three circles have traditionally defined the cycle of art among fine artists, such as painters and sculptors. I think these circles can work for anyone giving a gift or making a change in the world.

The first circle represents true gifts—items that an artist gleefully and willingly shares. This circle comprises friends or family or the people you work with. Someone comes over for dinner and you don't charge them. The meal is a gift. Friends ask for a stock tip or accounting help. You don't charge them. It's a gift.

The second circle is the circle of commerce. In this circle are people and organizations that pay for your art. They pay for a souvenir edition or a poster or a speech. They pay for consulting or a house concert or a newsletter subscription. ConEd pays Paul to work on its gas lines, knowing that his gift of working well with people comes along for the ride.

And now, the Internet creates a third circle, the circle of your tribe, your followers, fans who may become friends. Friendlies. This circle is new. It's huge and it's important, because it enables you to enlarge the second circle and make more money, and because it enables you to affect more people and improve more lives.

Monet gave paintings to friends (the first circle) or sold them to collectors (the second circle).

These in turn were sold for very high prices, sometimes after his death. The paintings were resold to people who needed to possess them, or who wanted to resell them or to some way control them.

Those paintings hang in museums, where they can be seen for free (or a small donation) by the masses (the third circle).

This third circle changes art for all artists, forever. It means that you can share your gift with more people, cheaper and quicker, than ever before. When you focus on the second circle, when you work to charge more people more often, your art suffers. Instead, we profit most when we make the first and third circles as big as we can. Generosity generates income. This works whether you are selling paintings or innovation or a service.

Linus Torvalds worked hard on creating the Linux operating system. He did it for free and he did it largely for his friends. The Internet permitted him to jump to a third circle, a hundred million or more people around the world who benefit from his art, who participate in his tribe and follow his work.

As the third circle grows in size, the second circle takes care of itself. Linus and the core team responsible for Linux will never need to look for work again, because as you give more and more to the friendlies, the list of people willing to pay you to do your work always grows.

The Difference Between "If" and "And"

In a monetary exchange, we focus on "if." I will give you this *if* you give me that. The initial exchange depends on the promise of reciprocity, and doesn't occur without it. In a gift, we imply *and*. I will give you this *and* you will do something for someone else. I will give you this *and* my expectation is that you will change the way you feel.

The power lies in the creation of abundance. A trade leaves things as they were, with no external surplus. A gift always creates a surplus as it spreads.

Washing Rental Cars

My friend Julie used to say, "No one washes a rental car before they return it."

The reason should now be obvious: Avis is not a member of our tribe. I paid for the car, they got the money, they should wash it. It's a transaction.

Transactions distance parties from each other. The transaction establishes the rules of the engagement, and if it's not in the rules, you don't have to worry about it. If I eat in your restaurant tonight and pay my check, there's no obligation for me to return tomorrow or for you to send me a Christmas card. We had a deal, a deal's a deal (what a great expression), and we can move on. In many ways, this tribeless relationship brings a great deal of freedom to our commerce and allows things to grow and spread and change quite rapidly.

Consider the alternative: The bellboy who refuses a tip for helping an elderly customer. The doctor who drives out of her way to check on a patient even though it's her day off. The restaurant owner who sends out a few special dishes to a regular customer and refuses to charge for them.

In each case, the lack of a transaction created a bond between the giver and the recipient, and perhaps surprisingly, the giver usually comes out even further ahead.

Hyatt Hotels is now treating different customers differently. Since they know who their best customers are, they're working not to charge them more, but to give them more. They're setting out to randomly cover bar tabs, offer free massages, and provide other services that they could otherwise charge for. If they do it in a corporate, by-the-book way, it'll feel fake and will fail. But if they empower their employees to actually be generous, it can't help but work.

Gifts of Art

As we've seen, if there is no gift, there is no art. When art is created solely to be sold, it's only a commodity. A key element for the artist is the act of giving the art to someone in the tribe. (To be clear, an object or a canvas or a deliverable is not necessary for it to be art. Seeing the thing, hearing the thing, understanding the thing—that's enough for it to be art.)

If I give you a piece of art, then you can't and shouldn't be busy assigning a monetary value to it. To do so is to take away its magic. If flight attendants charged extra for smiles, or helping you with a bag or entertaining your kid, that wouldn't be a gift and it wouldn't be art. It would be emotional labor for hire.

If I give you a piece of art, you shouldn't be required to work hard to reciprocate, because reciprocation is an act of keeping score, which involves monetizing the art, not appreciating it.

When I come to your house for dinner, I shouldn't bring brownies merely because you asked me over to dinner. To do so devalues and disrespects your gift.

An acquaintance of mine always gives a cash gift when he attends weddings or bar mitzvahs. He makes out the check over dessert after the ceremony—and the amount of the check is directly related to the amount he thinks was spent on the catering. A steak dinner earns you a bigger wedding check. Sigh.

Or consider the family that exchanges cash at Christmas. If everyone is giving and getting the same amount, there's not much happening, is there?

The gift of art instantly creates a bond between the artist and the recipient. A priceless gift has been given, one that can never be valued monetarily or paid for or reciprocated. The benefit to the artist is the knowledge that you changed in some way, not that you will repay him. And so your only possible response is to make the tribe stronger.

When I treat you with respect or spend the time to try to change your mind, I am embracing you in the best way I can. If I touch you in any way, you then have two obligations: to make us closer, and to pass it on, to give a gift to another member of the tribe. Gifts don't demand immediate payment, but they have always included social demands within the tribe.

The Selfish By-product

Some people are gift givers by nature. They love their tribe, or they respect their art, and so they give. Not for an ulterior motive, but because it gives them joy.

Other people might need to consider the economic benefits first. These are people who were brainwashed by the last five hundred years of history, people who want to know what's in it for them, people who

believe *there ain't no such thing as a free lunch* and *every man for himself.*
These people have no art in their life because they're unable to give a
true gift. They want something in return. They want security or cash
or both.

The hardheaded selfish capitalists among us will enjoy the next
sentence:

Artists are indispensable linchpins.

Art is scarce; scarcity creates value. Gifts make tribes stronger. Organizations will always strive to replace replaceable elements with cheaper
substitutes. But generous artists aren't easily replaceable.

So artists are different.

If you give a gift, I hope you will do it because you respect your muse
and embrace your art. But, right now anyway, I'll settle for your simulat-
ing this behavior simply because you want to be the linchpin, the center
of the tribe, the source of our inspiration, and the one we all count on
to make a difference.

Some people think that you can't be generous until after you become
a success. They argue that they have to get theirs, and *then* they can go
ahead and give back. The astonishing fact is that the most successful
people in the world are those who don't do it for the money.

Old-school businesspeople argue for copyright and patent protection
and say, "I can't tell you my idea because I'm afraid you will steal it."
Old-school thinking is that you get paid first, you sign a contract, you
protect and defend and profit. They say, "Pay me."

Artists say, "Here."

Three Ways People Think About Gifts

1. Give me a gift!
2. Here's a gift; now you owe me, big-time.
3. Here's a gift, I love you.

The first two are capitalist misunderstandings of what it means to
give or receive a gift. The third is the only valid alternative on the list.

Sunny Bates and Metcalfe's Law

Bob Metcalfe invented the technology that allows computers to be wired up in a network. The Ethernet, as he called it, made him rich. He also coined Metcalfe's law, which made him famous.

Metcalfe's law says that the value of a network increases with the square of the number of nodes on the network. In English? It says that the more people who have a fax machine, the more fax machines are worth (one person with a fax is useless). The more people who use the Internet, the better it works. The more friends I have who use Twitter, the more the tool is worth to me. Connections are valuable in and of themselves, because they lead to productivity, decreased communication costs, and yes, gifts.

Sunny Bates is a human Ethernet. Sunny ran a very successful executive recruiting firm, sold it, and now creates value by helping clients connect to relevant communities. Her job is to connect people. The connections she creates require emotional labor on her part. She risks rejection. She has to engage with people who might not like her right away, or she must engage with ideas that challenge her. The magic of her art is that this gift continues to multiply. As her network increases, more value is created. Sunny rarely charges for what she does, because the gift nature of her work is what makes it so powerful (and because she loves the work).

The Magic of Living Below Your Means

One of the reasons people give for not giving gifts is that they can't afford it. Gifts don't have to cost money, but they always cost time and effort. If you're in a panic about money, those two things are hard to find. The reason these people believe they can't afford it, though, is that they've so bought into consumer culture that they're in debt or have monthly bills that make no sense at all.

When you cut your expenses to the bone, you have a surplus. The surplus allows you to be generous, which mysteriously turns around and makes your surplus even bigger.

How to Receive a Gift

It's possible to destroy an artist by refusing his gifts.

It's possible to destroy him by wasting his gifts as well, or by receiving them in the wrong way.

Hollywood kills artists every day. They find an independent film-maker who has made a wonderful gift of a film. Then they buy him off, give him too much money and not enough freedom, and choke him to death. The record industry destroys artists regularly by forcing them to conform in exchange for the promise that they will spread the gift of their art.

Why, precisely, is that customer service rep going the extra mile? What's in it for her to deliver a gift so precious when she's not in line for extra cash? Cash-focused, short-term profit seekers can't bear this. They don't want a relationship that isn't based on money, and they want to be able to turn the art on or off at will.

For some artists, the benefits are all internal. Creating art is an intrinsic good, something they enjoy. They don't want anything, don't seek anything, and if they're particularly resolute, won't get anything.

Most artists, though, are seeking some sort of feedback. They want to know that the art they are creating is causing a change, that it's *working*.

And some artists want fame and fortune.

Every artist I've ever met wants to build bonds, wants to cause connections to be made.

Do you think that Bob Dylan wants fans stalking him, wants to be treated awkwardly wherever he goes, wants to be invited to your kid's birthday party because you know a friend of a friend of his son's? Dylan doesn't want to be your friend, he wants to cause you to change or connect.

Do you think the innovative kid in the mailroom wants a fifty-dollar check in his pay envelope as payment for the new system he pushed for that saves the company a million dollars a year? Is that why he did it?

A gift well received can lead to more gifts. But artists don't give gifts for money. They do it for respect and connection and to cause change. So the best recipients are the ones who can reciprocate in kind. With honest gratitude. With clear reports about change that was created. With gifts that actually cost us, not just a tiny gratuity or faux appreciation.

Manipulation of the Gift Economy

As soon as you draw the map and mechanize and monetize emotional labor, you ruin it.

The pasted-on smiles of a guide at Disney World, for example, have far less power than the genuine connection a tourist makes—even for an instant—with a blue-collar worker manning the controls of the ride.

That's why telemarketers who read scripts never achieve the results of salespeople who actually speak what they believe. As big business has realized that people crave connection, not stuff, they've tried to institutionalize it, measure it, and reward it. And they fail every time.

Think of the flight attendant standing at the exit to the plane, saying "B'bye, B'bye" over and over again, doing it because she must, not because she wants to.

The intent of the giver and the posture of the recipient are critical. I'm not arguing that you must fake your attitude and cop a new behavior in order to get ahead.

Working the first-class cabin at British Airways can be a nightmare job. Spoiled, tired executives are waited on by flight attendants for hours on end, rarely earning the service they demand. Sure, they paid for it, but all too often, they're not open or receptive to it.

The secret of working this flight, I've been told by the people who do the work, is to realize that the extraordinary service being delivered is not for the passenger, and it's not for British Airways. It's for the flight attendant.

The most successful givers aren't doing it because they're being told to. They do it because doing it is fun. It gives them joy.

Sure, it would be better if they got paid a fair wage, and it would be a lot better if more passengers appreciated their work. But until those two things happen, the most successful and happiest flight attendants will be embracing their art, not looking for someone to applaud them. If their airline started using hidden cameras and customer report forms to push them to do it more, they'd actually do it less. Manipulated art (even the art of service) ceases to be art.

Great bosses and world-class organizations hire motivated people, set high expectations, and give their people room to become remarkable.

The Internet as a Gift System

I hesitate to use the phrase "gift economy" because as soon as I do, people wonder what they're going to get and how much they'll have to pay for it.

Clay Shirky and Doug Rushkoff have both talked about the public gift nature of the 'Net. Someone puts a video up on YouTube; why? No obvious revenue potential, no ad sales, no clear path to fame. It's a gift.

At first, gifts you can give live in a tiny realm. You do something for yourself, or for a friend or two. Soon, though, the circle of the gift gets bigger. The Internet gives you leverage. A hundred people read your blog, or fifty subscribe to your podcast. There's no economy here, but there is an audience, a chance to share your gift.

And that circle begets other circles. The audience you charmed with your video realizes that they too can give a gift to the community. And so they do. And the audience continues to grow, each person enjoying the digital fruits of the labor that others donate to the ever-widening circle.

The fact that there's no organized cash or exchange system is part of what makes it work. If I send you two links and then you feel obligated to send me two links, we don't have art; we have an economy of reciprocity.

I don't write my blog to get anything from you in exchange. I write it because giving my small gift to the community in the form of writing makes me feel good. I enjoy it that you enjoy it. When that gift comes back to me, one day, in an unexpected way, I enjoy the work I did twice as much.

Reciprocity defined as payment for my work isn't the point. It's the appreciation of my work, the way it changes people—that's my payment.

The Internet has taken the idea of gifts, multiplied it, and then pushed it into a realm where gifts previously hadn't had much traction. The gift system is now a bigger part of commerce than it ever has been before.

Margaret Thatcher famously said, "There is no such thing as society." While this is ridiculous on its face, the enlarging circle of gift culture demonstrates how false this statement is in practice. *Society is where we give gifts.*

Someone in your office publishes a paper about a new technique, or gives a talk at a conference for no pay. You go the extra mile to please a small customer, or build an online forum to teach your customers how to get more out of your products (for no extra cost). These are all examples of the gift system at work. It works even more profoundly on an internal basis. Someone who is not in your department steps in and helps out during a crunch. A coworker shares his address book. You brainstorm a new idea with another salesperson. In each case, there's no reciprocity, no guarantee of repayment. Instead, there's an ever-enlarging circle, a circle where gifts are valued and passed on.

The only people who don't benefit from this are the hoarders. People who take gifts but don't give them find themselves temporarily ahead of the game, but ultimately left out.

Sometimes, I Don't Want Your Gift

The thing about reciprocity and the system of gifts is that it demands that the recipient participate. The humanity of the interaction leaves little room for someone to opt out, to remain isolated, or to hoard. If you take that posture, your circle gets smaller.

For the system to function, all sides have to opt in, both giving and getting.

Your boss might not want her status quo changed. Your harried customer might not want his day brightened. Your co-worker might not want to change everything.

And this is the challenge of becoming the linchpin. Not only must you be an artist, must you be generous, and must you be able to see where you can help, but you must also be aware. Aware of where your skills are welcomed.

The street performer is a great metaphor for you and your work. She stands on the corner, busking for tips. Most people walk by. *That's fine.* If someone walks by, changing your act to attract her or running after her is a foolish game. The performer seeks the people who *choose* to stop and watch and interact and ultimately donate.

Great work is not created for everyone. If it were, it would be average work.

"Thank You and . . ."

If you appreciate a gift, consider saying, "thank you and . . ."

Thank you and I dog-eared forty of the pages.

Thank you and I told your boss what a wonderful thing you did.

Thank you and here's a record my band and I recorded last week.

Thank you and you made me cry.

Thank you and I just blogged about what you did.

Thank you and here's a twenty-dollar tip; I know it's not much, but it's all I can afford right now.

Thank you and how can I help you spread the word?

Thank you and can you teach me how to do that?

Thank you and you changed me, forever.

How to Encourage Gifts

The gift giver may be intrinsically motivated, in which case she's doing it for herself, not for you or your organization. But either way, what people delivering gifts seek is respect.

Money isn't the way to show respect. Money is an essential element of making a living in this world, but money is a poor substitute for respect and thanks. Wall Street has learned this the hard way.

When someone in your organization starts acting like a linchpin, order in lunch for the team, in his honor.

When someone delivers more than you asked, give her more trust, more freedom, more leeway next time.

When someone gives a speech that exceeds the bar, don't merely circle three 5s on the conference speaker review sheets. Instead, give him a standing ovation, wait to thank him after the talk, tell ten friends what you saw, and thank the conference organizer. It wasn't a transaction that you pay for with a few circles on a review sheet. It was a gift. If you want to repay it, do something difficult.

When a volunteer really steps up in your political campaign, don't just mumble a "thanks" at the beginning of your next speech. Call her at home the next day and say thank you. Put her picture on your Web site. Insist on getting a photo shot with the two of you.

Respect is the gift you can offer in return.

You Can Rip Off an Artist Only Once

Let me be really clear: I'm not suggesting that artists shouldn't get paid. They should, and a lot.

But the nature of a gift means that a quid pro quo doesn't really work. "Do this and I'll pay you" is a contract, not a way of creating art.

The artist is producing a gift, making a change, causing good things to happen without hope for repayment. So, it's possible to give less than you get from someone who is generous. For a while. But smart people don't tolerate this for long, and the marketplace values these rare people too highly for this inequity to be a long-term solution for capitalists. If you are lucky enough to work with someone this generous, pay him a lot, or your competition will.

Slow down and think that one through. If you are fortunate enough to find an artist, you should work hard to pay him as much as you can afford, because if you don't, someone else will.

But How!?

How do I know what art to make? How do I know what gifts to give?

This is the crux of it. Once you commit to being an artist, the question is an obvious one. The answer is the secret to your success. You must make a map.

Not someone else. You.

THERE IS NO MAP

The Linchpin, the Artist, and the Map

You must become indispensable to thrive in the new economy. The best ways to do that are to be remarkable, insightful, an artist, someone bearing gifts. To lead. The worst way is to conform and become a cog in a giant system.

What does it take to lead?

The key distinction is the ability to forge your own path, to discover a route from one place to another that hasn't been paved, measured, and quantified. So many times we want someone to tell us exactly what to do, and so many times that's exactly the wrong approach.

Diamond cutters have an intrinsic understanding of the stone in their hands. They can touch and see exactly where the best lines are; they *know*. The greatest artists do just that. They see and understand the challenges before them, without carrying the baggage of expectations or attachment. The diamond cutter doesn't imagine the diamond he wants. Instead, he sees the diamond that is possible.

Seeing, Discernment, and *Prajna*

You can't make a map unless you can see the world as it is. You have to know where you are and know where you're going before you can figure out how to go about getting there.

No one has a transparent view of the world. In fact, we all carry around a personal worldview—the biases and experiences and expectations that color the way we perceive the world.

The venture capitalist has a worldview shaped by his experience in funding dozens of companies over the years. He remembers the last bubble and the bubble before that, and he has the scars to prove it. So when you show him your business plan, he doesn't see only your plan. He also sees the echoes of past plans. He remembers other people, other days, other ventures. And those memories color his perception.

The loyal employee has a worldview as well. She wants a stable place to work, and she believes in you. So when you show her your plan, her worldview changes her feelings and her analysis of your plan.

And the lawyer and the competitor and the skeptic and the mother-in-law each have their own worldviews, their own biases and expectations. None of us knows the absolute truth, of course, but the goal is to approach a situation with the least possible bias.

So the manager and the investor seek out an employee with discernment, the ability to see things as they truly are. A Buddhist might call this *prajna*. A life without attachment and stress can give you the freedom to see things as they are and call them as you see them. If you had this skill, what an asset you would be to any organization.

Of course, no one does this all the time. When we apply to college, we're attached to the outcome, so we're blinded to the reality of the process. When our company does layoffs, we're attached to the outcome, so we're blinded by the truth of the situation. Over and over, in the moments when we need to see our options the most clearly, we get stuck.

Seeing Clearly Isn't Easy

It's difficult work, which is why it's so rare and valuable.

Seeing clearly means being able to look at a business plan from the point of view of the investor, the entrepreneur, and the market. That's hard.

Seeing clearly means being able to do a job interview as though you weren't the interviewer or the applicant, but someone watching dispassionately from a third chair.

Seeing clearly means that you're smart enough to know when a project is doomed, or brave enough to persevere when your colleagues are fleeing for the hills.

Abandoning your worldview in order to try on someone else's is the first step in being able to see things as they are.

Annoyed at Intent

The car across the street won't stop honking its horn. Not the car, actually, but the person in the car. I can't get a thing done, it's so annoying.

The next night, the wind is blowing hard. Every few minutes, a leaf or twig hits my window. It's sort of comforting knowing that I'm safe inside. I work away.

What's the difference?

I'm giving a talk. The microphone stops working. The overworked guy in the stage crew forgot to change the batteries before I started. I'm annoyed. Almost angry. Right now, I'm not thinking about how overworked he is, or how many things he had to do. I'm thinking about how evil he was, how he deliberately sabotaged me for no reason. All this hard work, sabotaged by a careless error. I walk over and pick up the backup microphone, but my rhythm is shot.

A few weeks later, another talk. The bulb in the projector burns out midway through. Couldn't be helped. A hiccup of nature. I don't miss a beat and finish the talk without the slides.

Equanimity is easy when we're dealing with a random event. Stuff happens. We don't get angry at birds chirping or even a thunderstorm occurring during a play. But if a cell phone goes off, that's an entirely different story. We need to sit and seethe, as if that seething is magically sending horrible vibes to the offender and *he will never do it again*.

The linchpin understands that getting angry about the battery in the microphone isn't going to make the battery come back to life. And teaching the stage-crew guy a lesson is senseless and not going to help much, either. So you deal with it.

If you accept that human beings are difficult to change, and embrace (rather than curse) the uniqueness that everyone brings to the table, you'll navigate the world with more bliss and effectiveness. And make better decisions, too.

Teaching Fire a Lesson

Fire is hot. That's what it does. If you get burned by fire, you can be annoyed at yourself, but being angry at the fire doesn't do you much good. And trying to teach the fire a lesson so it won't be hot next time is certainly not time well spent.

Our inclination is to give fire a pass, because it's not human. But human beings are similar, in that they're not going to change any time soon either.

And yet, many (most?) people in organizations handle their interactions as though they are in charge of teaching people a lesson. We make policies and are vindictive and focus on the past because we worry that if we don't, someone will get away with it.

So when a driver cuts us off, we scream and yell. We say we're doing it so he'll learn and not endanger the next guy, but of course, he can't hear you. There's a media mogul who stole from me in 1987 and I haven't spoken to him since. He doesn't even know I exist, I bet. So much for teaching him a lesson.

The ability to see the world as it is begins with an understanding that perhaps it's not your job to change what can't be changed. Particularly if the act of working on that change harms you and your goals in the process.

Elements of Attachment

The first sign of attachment is that you try to use telekinesis and mind control to remotely control what other people think of you and your work. We've all done this.

You work really hard on something, or you debut a special project, or there's a particularly important meeting. You've done everything you can, and now the crowd is deciding on its reaction. Are you wrinkling your forehead and willing them to make a choice? The focused energy of brainpower mind control is exhausting and completely ineffective.

You will exhaust yourself in this effort, and it will never work. No one ever says, "I'm glad I spent hours turning this situation over and over in my mind last night, because it prepared me for today's meeting."

The second sign of attachment is how you handle bad news. If bad news changes your emotional state or what you think of yourself, then you'll be attached to the outcome you receive. The alternative is to ask, "Isn't that interesting?" Learn what you can learn; then move on.

We do this all the time, of course. You're playing pinball on a new pinball machine and you see that the left flipper doesn't work the way you expect it will. You don't have an emotional meltdown when the ball drains. No, you notice it, you learn from it, and your next ball goes better. You have discernment. You can see what's happening and you can learn from it. The flipper isn't about you, and the ball draining down the hole is not a personal attack. It just is.

Interactions in the real world often feel more complex than a pinball machine. We assign motivations and plots and vendettas where there are none. Those angry customers didn't wake up this morning deciding to ruin your day, not at all. They're just angry. It's not personal and it's not rational and it certainly isn't about whether or not you deserve it. It just is. So now what are you going to do about it?

When our responses turn into reactions and we set out to teach people a lesson, we lose. We lose because the act of teaching someone a lesson rarely succeeds at changing them, and always fails at making our day better, or our work more useful.

The Two Reasons Seeing the Future Is So Difficult

Attachment to an outcome combined with the resistance and fear of change.

That's it.

You have all the information that everyone else has. But if you are deliberately trying to create a future that feels safe, you will willfully ignore the future that is likely.

Yelling at the Ref

Tony is a professional sportscaster, and a good one. He can call a game on the radio with such energy and detail that you feel as if you're there. He sees what's happening and lets you know.

In his spare time, Tony loves pickup basketball. On the court, his discernment disappears. A bad call enrages him. He screams and gets uptight. Every call feels as though it is against him and his team, and he's sure that the ref is losing the game for him. It can take him five minutes to settle back into his game.

The essential question of *prajna* is what to do about the ref. If you filter the calls through your partisan point of view, of course you'll be upset. Who wouldn't be? The challenge is determining if that filter is helping you thrive.

If you're able to look at what's happening in your world and say, "There's the pattern," or "Wow, that's interesting, I wonder why," then you're far more likely to respond productively than if your reaction is "How dare he!"

Effort Can Change Things

One of the fascinating aspects of business and organized movements is that there's some correlation between the passion and effort that people bring to a project and the outcome.

This isn't true for the weather. Accept the day's forecast for what it is, because there's nothing you can do about it. But market share, innovation, negotiations, human relations—they can be shifted with the right sort of insight and effort.

The challenge is in understanding when our effort can't possibly be enough, and in choosing projects and opportunities that are most likely to reward the passion we bring to a situation. If there's no way in the world you can please that customer with a reasonable amount of effort, perhaps it's better to accept the situation than it is to kill yourself trying (and failing) to change that person's mindset.

There's a difference between passively accepting every element of your environment (and thus missing opportunities to exploit) and being wise enough to leave the unchangeable alone, or at least work around it.

Zen at the Airport

You can learn a lot at a full-service counter at the airport, particularly on a snowy day.

Some travelers are adroit at navigating the outcomes dealt to them by weather and scheduling snafus. Others completely melt down. And the result of the emotional crash is that these travelers do a poor job of making new plans.

The woman in front of me isn't going to make it to her flight to Florida. Planes leave, planes don't leave. There's nothing she can do about this. But she's unable to accept the world as it is, so she has a meltdown. Instead of calmly looking at the situation, quickly switching to a different airline, and moving on (which would have led to her arriving in Palm Beach only ten minutes late), she needs to deny the truth about her flight and the motivation of the person who canceled it. Then she needs someone to blame. Her emotional connection to the outcome blinds her to the choices that are available to her.

In this moment, she had a choice. She could remain attached to the outcome she was in hate with, or she could have a moment of *prajna*, an acceptance of the world as it is, regardless of how she wants it to be.

Forty years ago, Richard Branson, who ultimately founded Virgin Air, found himself in a similar situation in an airport in the Caribbean. They had just canceled his flight, the only flight that day. Instead of freaking out about how essential the flight was, how badly his day was ruined, how his entire career was now in jeopardy, the young Branson walked across the airport to the charter desk and inquired about the cost of chartering a flight out of Puerto Rico.

Then he borrowed a portable blackboard and wrote, "Seats to Virgin Islands, $39." He went back to his gate, sold enough seats to his fellow passengers to completely cover his costs, and made it home on time. Not to mention planting the seeds for the airline he'd start decades later. Sounds like the kind of person you'd like to hire.

The Quadrants of Discernment

On one axis is passion. The other, attachment.

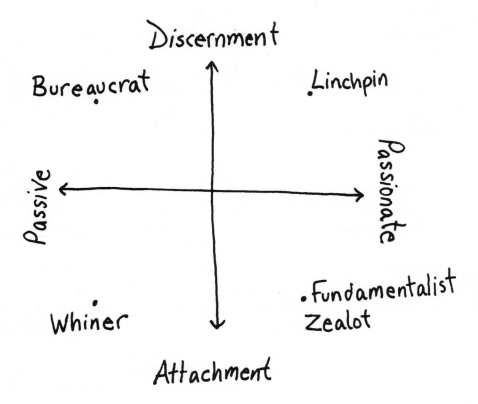

Each corner represents a different kind of person and the way he responds to situations at work.

In the bottom right is the Fundamentalist Zealot. He is attached to the world as he sees it. There is no *prajna* here, no discernment. Change is a threat. Curiosity is a threat. Competition is a threat. As a result, it's difficult for him to see the world as it is, because he insists on the world being the way he imagines it. At the same time, he has huge reservoirs of effort to invest in maintaining his worldview. Fundamentalist zealots always manage to make the world smaller, poorer, and meaner.

The RIAA's campaign to sue people for listening to music online is the work of the fundamentalist zealot. The organization spent hundreds of millions of dollars suing people around the world, despite clear evidence that their efforts weren't working and couldn't possibly succeed. The combination of attachment (to the world as they wanted it to be) and passion (to spend time and money to ensure this) was both risky and wasteful.

The top left belongs to the Bureaucrat. He's certainly not attached to the outcome of events, and he definitely won't be exerting any additional effort, regardless. The bureaucrat is a passionless rules follower, indifferent to external events and gliding through the day. The clerk at the post office and the exhausted VP at General Motors are both bureaucrats.

The bottom left is the corner for the Whiner. The whiner has no passion, but is extremely attached to the worldview he's bought into. Living life in fear of change, the whiner can't muster the effort to make things better, but is extremely focused on wishing that things stay as they are. I'd put most people in the newspaper industry in this corner. They stood by for years, watching the industry crumble while they resolutely did nothing except whine about unfairness. Almost all the positive change in this industry (like *The Huffington Post* and YouTube) is coming from outsiders.

And that leaves the top right, the quadrant of the Linchpin. The linchpin is enlightened enough to see the world as it is, to understand that this angry customer is not about me, that this change in government policy is not a personal attack, that this job is not guaranteed for life. At the same time, the linchpin brings passion to the job. She knows from experience that the right effort in the right place *can* change the outcome, and she reserves her effort for doing just that.

The linchpin has no time or energy for whining or litigation. Instead, she's obsessively focused on the projects that have a likelihood of changing the outcome.

Here's another way to describe the two axes: One asks, *Can you see it?* The other wonders, *Do you care?*

Someone Else, Please Be in Charge

My flight home was recently diverted to Albany, New York. We were stuck at the gate, held hostage by the airline with a prognosis of a delay that would last somewhere from ninety minutes to five hours. Experienced travelers know that when the system breaks, it's broken. Bail!

I persuaded the flight attendant to give me permission to leave the plane. I had already gone online and found a rental car for forty dollars. The drive to the airport in White Plains was about 130 minutes. Clearly this was a good bet.

I stood up to leave and said to the other twenty-three passengers, "I'm leaving and driving to the White Plains airport. We'll be there in about two hours. If you want to join me, I have room for four other people, and it's free."

No one moved. I drove myself home.

I've thought about that a lot. Some of these people may have figured I was some sort of extremely well-dressed business-traveler psychopath. My guess, though, is that most of them were very content to blame United for their situation. If they had stood up and left the plane, the situation would have belonged to them. Their choice, their responsibility.

Self-defense

When you defend your position, what are you defending?

Are you defending your past, your present, or the future you are nostalgic about?

The market doesn't care about your defense. It cares about working with someone who can accurately see what was, what is, and where things are headed. When you see a bump up ahead, do you say, "Oh my god we're doomed!" or do you say, "Isn't that interesting?"

When a vendor or a customer must choose between an organization working hard to defend the status quo and one that's open to big growth in the future, the choice is pretty simple.

There's no shortage of panic and no shortage of people willing to rearrange the truth to preserve their vision of the world as they'd like it to be. There are lobbyists in Washington who make a great living helping corporations fight the inevitable future by arguing for protection. There are nonprofits that have long lost their reason to exist, but are still maintained by management that doesn't have the guts to admit the world has passed them by. The same mindset that drives someone to stay in their home during a hurricane is at work. Just because you want something to be true doesn't make it so.

Scarcity creates value, and what's scarce is a desire to accept what is and then work to change it for the better, not deny that it exists.

The Artist and *Prajna*

Worldview and attachment always color perceptions. Ask people in the customer service department about the biggest problem the company faces, and they will almost certainly define the challenge in terms of customer service. Ask the same question of the guys in finance, and of course, the answer will be based on the financial lens they use to see the world.

Artists can't get attached to the object of their attention. The attachment to a worldview changes an artist's relationship to what's happening and prevents him from converting what he sees or interacts with into something that belongs to him, that he can work with and change.

A brilliant negotiator does her art by understanding the other side as honestly as anyone can. Only by seeing the world through clear eyes can she possibly craft a negotiation strategy that works for everyone.

It's very easy for us to become attached to our feelings and memories and expectations of the system we work in, the companies we invest in, the people we work with. That attachment, and our response to it, forces us to wish for a different outcome than we might honestly expect.

The executives in the record business, for example, loved their perfect business model. They were attached to their lifestyles and to the way their artist and fan relationships made them feel. When even a turnip could see that their business model was doomed, they soldiered on, apparently oblivious to the crumbling going on around them. Were they stupid? No. They were blinded by their attachment to the present and their fear of the future.

Bob Lefsetz, the iconic critic of the industry, was the outsider who could actually see the future. On a regular basis, he told the thousands of executives who subscribed to his newsletter exactly what was happening and why it was happening. More than five years ago, he was (loudly) calling for the music industry to wake up or die. Bob's art is his ability with words, his willingness to see the truth and reflect it to people who might not want to hear it.

Executives disappeared, but Bob remained indispensable. Because he was the only truth-teller in the room, many influential players in the industry quickly realized that they would have trouble living without him, even if they didn't like the future he was so accurately describing. So Bob makes his living speaking truth to power.

Untangling the Truth

Successful people are able to see the threads of the past and the threads of the future and untangle them into something manageable.

The tangling is a natural state. Personalities, sunk costs, and complex systems conspire to weave the elements of our work into a matted mess. Things are the way they are, and it's difficult to perceive that they could be any other way.

The newspaper industry can't untangle news from paper, can't see the difference between delivering the news around the world for free and putting it on a truck for shipment down the block. As long as each of these elements is seen as inseparable from the others, it's impossible to untangle the future. That's why outsiders and insurgents so often invent the next big thing—they don't start with the tangled past.

The truth behind your customer's situation is no different. Your organization may have a history with this customer; you may have a visceral memory of something that happened between or with your organization and the customer. Keep these ideas tangled and there's no way you'll be flexible enough to partner with this customer for the future. You'll be too busy defending the past.

Tell the Truth

First, of course, you have to be able to see the truth. This takes experience and expertise and, most of all, a willingness to look.

Most people who see the truth refuse to acknowledge it. We can notice an unhappy customer, a shoddy product, or a decaying industry, but we don't want to be aware of it. Our attachment is to a different future, so we ignore the data or diminish its importance. We don't mean to lie; we're in denial.

The few who can see the truth and become aware of it often hesitate to speak up. You don't want to upset the status quo. You fear the wrath of your peers when they hear you say that the emperor is actually naked. You hesitate because you've been taught that this is not the work of a team player; it's the work of a rabble-rouser.

Smart organizations seek out people with the ability to see the world as it actually is. But that skill is worthless if you don't acknowledge the truth and share it.

Think of the travel agents you know who denied that the industry was in trouble until it disappeared. Or the sales rep with a fading account who stuck it out because momentum was more important than acknowledging the truth. It's human nature to defend our worldview, to construct a narrative that protects us from uncomfortable confessions.

Attachment to Things We Can't Control

At this moment, your boss is meeting with the board to determine whether or not to renew your contract.

Precisely how much worrying is appropriate? If you devote an enormous number of conscious brain cycles to willing, wishing, and wanting the meeting to come out a certain way, will it help? What if you devote *all* of your mental power to it? Still doesn't work.

The linchpin has figured out that we get only a certain number of brain cycles to spend each day. Spending even one on a situation out of our control has a significant opportunity cost. Your competition is busy allocating time to create the future, and you are stuck wishing the world was different. We're attached to a certain view, a given outcome, and when it doesn't appear, we waste time mourning the world that we wanted that isn't here.

When an angry customer is standing at the counter, we can curse his poor judgment or the world that brought him to us, but the linchpin has figured out that accepting the situation and improving it clearly beats the alternative.

Scientists Are Mapmakers

Lab assistants do what they're told. Scientists figure out what to do next.

It's not a surprise when a scientist is surprised. That's what happens when she is doing her job properly. To explore, to follow hunches, to see the landscape and plot a new course. Setting yourself up to be surprised is a conscious choice.

Scientists never believe that it's all figured out, totally settled. They understand that there's always another argument or mystery around the corner, which means that the map is never perfected.

Craig Venter, who first decoded the human genome, didn't wait for someone to tell him what to do next.

Figuring out what to do next was his contribution as a linchpin.

The Guild of Frustrated Artists

One of my favorite negative reviews of my book *Tribes*:

"Godin doesn't explain how to go about doing the actual hard groundwork of leadership. He makes it sound like anyone with an idea and a cell phone can rally thousands of people to their cause in minutes if they just realize that it's not hard."

My response: Telling people leadership is important is one thing. Showing them step by step precisely how to be a leader is impossible. "Tell me what to do" is a nonsensical statement in this context.

There is no map. No map to be a leader, no map to be an artist. I've read hundreds of books about art (in all its forms) and how to do it, and not one has a clue about the map, because there isn't one.

Here's the truth that you have to wrestle with: the reason that art (writing, engaging, leading, all of it) is valuable is precisely why I can't tell you how to do it. If there were a map, there'd be no art, because art is the act of navigating without a map.

Don't you hate that? I love that there's no map.

The Endless Emergency of Fitting In

It's never possible to fit all the way in. Never possible for everything to be all right.

How can it ever be?

And so we're trapped, always seeking to fit in a little more, always looking for one more signal that we haven't gotten it just right, that the system is about to be disrupted, that the rules will change again and that we'll have to adjust (again).

The problem with being outwardly focused is that we have no center, nothing to return to. The problem with outward focus is that there is no compass, no normal, no way to tell if we're in balance.

Without a map, how can we know what's next?

In *The Lonely Crowd*, David Riesman writes, "Americans were ready for the mass media even before the mass media were ready for them." We needed the cues and instructions, and yes, the map, in order to figure out who we should be.

MAKING THE CHOICE

Impossible, Yes, So Let's Get to Work

The merest attempt at estimating, the slightest unconscious recording is shrugged off as an absurd association with some never-to-be-realized dream . . . as an exercise in futility . . .

I manage to whisper my first thought (whisper, so the demons won't hear): "I know it's impossible. But I know I'll do it."

At that instant, the towers become "my towers."

Once on the street, a new thought: Impossible, yes, so let's get to work.

—from *Man on Wire*, a must-read diary of tightrope walker Philippe Petit's conquest of the World Trade Center

Everything you've been taught, everything you believe, is upended by the artist in Philippe Petit.

You don't engage in breaking and entering, you don't mount a major trespass, you don't risk your life, you certainly don't do it for no money, you don't dedicate your life to accomplishing something manifestly stupid and simultaneously beautiful. Most of all, you don't set out to do something impossible. Certainly not as a gift.

Unless you do.

And then you win.

Getting a New Job Without Leaving

One day, Binny Thomas stood up.

She stood up, spoke up, and started doing a new job. She didn't leave her organization, didn't even get a new title or new responsibilities. Instead, she started doing her old job in a new way. Binny stopped going to meetings with the goal of finding deniability or problems to avoid. Instead, she started leaning in and seeking out projects where she could make a difference.

Suddenly, Binny was inspired. She was looking for opportunities instead of hiding from blame. She was putting herself on the line, pushing through the dip, and making things happen. The fascinating (and universal) truth is that the opportunities came *after* she was inspired— she wasn't inspired by the opportunities.

Binny's old job was just fine. She did it extremely well. She followed the map, followed instructions, did what she was told and got paid what she was worth. Binny wasn't in danger of losing her job, but she had already given up her soul. She had plateaued, this was the end. Then she changed her mind.

Six weeks later, she got a huge promotion and another, even better new job than the new job she had given herself. Binny is now running a worldwide program of motivated scholars. All it took was a choice. Binny didn't ask for permission to do her job better; she merely decided to.

The Banker to the Amish

Bill O'Brien is the most beloved banker in Lancaster County, Pennsylvania. He is the leading banker to the Amish community there, and he says he's never lost a single house to foreclosure.

Bill isn't Amish, but most of his customers are. He manages more than $100 million worth of loans for HomeTowne Heritage Bank, and at least $90 million of that is in mortgages for Amish farms.

O'Brien drives more than a thousand miles a week, visiting his customers and prospective borrowers. They have no credit history, none of the usual tools of his business. "I'll find out who his dad was," he says.

"I'm also interested in who his wife's father was. It takes a team to make a farm go."

Part of the reason that his loan-and-hold approach is so successful is that he doesn't have much choice. He's legally forbidden from reselling the loans, because the houses have no electricity and no traditional homeowners insurance. As a result, if HomeTowne makes a loan, HomeTowne owns the loan.

That means that over the years, Bill has ended up on a first-name basis with almost all of his customers. Here's a banker who's making millions of dollars a year for his bank, doing business face to face and making each connection *more* human, not less.

New business is easy to find. The Amish community remains tightly knit, and when a new farm is purchased, the family buying it can't help but hear all about Bill. It wouldn't take very much to undo all this positive word of mouth, and as a result, Bill holds himself even more accountable.

Bill doesn't own the bank. But he's indispensable. The asset that Bill has built goes far beyond his book of business. He's a linchpin for his bank and for the Amish as well.

John Sells Insurance

I was standing at the bar of a hotel, killing time, drinking club soda and chatting with the bartender before I went on stage to give a speech. It turns out that he was a full-time insurance salesman moonlighting as a bartender to make ends meet. He sold insurance to small businesses, door to door.

John was a veteran, recently back from Iraq. I was interested in his charisma and proud of his service, so we chatted. The amount of emotional labor he put into his work was obvious, and, fascinated that people were still selling things door to door, I asked him about his day and his compensation. It turns out that 100 percent of his income was in commissions, and the company didn't really give him leads. Even worse, the company required him to use their business cards, their materials, and their script, at his expense. Not a perfect job, and certainly someone with

John's interpersonal skills could do better. He was putting himself on the line, essentially acting as human spam, and getting paid a pittance to do it.

I started to give him some ideas on how he could gather better leads, how he could be more remarkable in his presentation, how he could turn a few casual customers into a larger group of truly committed customers.

Then John surprised me. He explained that he didn't want to risk anything that might work better, didn't want to leverage his time, didn't want to do anything except follow the rules. If he worked long enough and hard enough, he assured me, the system would pay off for him. He had gone from risking his life in the desert with IEDs to being afraid of a new way of selling insurance.

This upset me. Of course John has a right to run his commission-based career any way he wants to. It's his choice. But John has been brainwashed, sold hard on not becoming a linchpin. His boss has given him a script, a set of rules, and has intimidated him into leaving his art at home. As a result, he ends up as a follower, a cog, a quiet, replaceable participant in the system.

The problem is that the system is ripping him off. He's not getting compensated fairly. He's doing what he's told and it's not working. To deal with all the rejection and to have that work be unrewarded isn't fair. He's 90 percent of the way to superstar status—all that's missing is the desire to create forward motion, to stand out and not merely fit in.

Just because his boss demands that he act like human spam doesn't mean he has an obligation to listen. In fact, he has an obligation to do just the opposite. To stand out, not to fit in. To make connections, not to be an invisible cog. To do otherwise is a loss.

Someone like John shouldn't have to moonlight to pay the bills.

Who Sets Your Agenda?

Who is your boss? What is your work for? Whom are you trying to please?

If you are working only for the person you report to according to the org chart, you may be sacrificing your future. Pleasing him may cause you to alienate customers, hide your best work, fit in, and become merely a cog in the system. The system wants you to fit in, but pleasing the system may not be your real work.

The typical big college in the United States today has a binge culture. The agenda is to get by in class, party a lot, become popular, and drink when you can. It's not so difficult to adopt this agenda, not so difficult to fit in. But where does it get you?

The typical nonprofit has embraced its status quo. If you embrace it, too, you'll get no pushback. Your anxieties will be minimized and your fears will not be aroused. But what will it lead to?

Your hard-charging boss wants to look good, and he's going to do this by cutting short-term costs. You can help him by doing nothing all day, spending no money, and making no noise. Then what happens?

If your agenda is set by someone else and it doesn't lead you where you want to go, why is it your agenda?

The Candyland Decree

Author Steven Johnson hates the board game Candyland and all board games like it. I hate them even more than he does.

"I realize that games of pure chance have a long history, but that doesn't make them any less moronic," he writes. Here's how Candyland is played: You pick a card and do what it says. Repeat.

This is early training in agenda following. Indoctrination in obedience. We teach kids that the best way to win is to mindlessly pick cards, follow instructions, and wait for it all to turn out okay.

Sheesh. What a disaster.

My decree: If you own a copy, burn it. Replace it with Cosmic Encounter or chess or a big box filled with wooden blocks. Please don't look at school or even board games the same way again. If they're teaching your kids or future employees to be map readers and agenda followers, make them stop.

Looking for Something to React or Respond To

In the old-school factory, the twin taskmasters are the manual and the assembly line.

The manual tells you what to do, and the assembly line keeps the work coming. It's not your job to decide.

When we moved away from assembly and manual labor, it was easy to pretend that we were no longer working in a factory. It turns out that our work changed, but our psyches didn't.

Now, we go looking for something to distract us. That's the culture of the Internet, combined with the culture of the white-collar cubicle worker, combined with fear.

You don't want to take initiative or responsibility, so you check your incoming mail, your Twitter stream, and your blog comments. Surely, there's something to play off of, something to get angry about, some meeting to go to. I know someone who goes to forty conferences a year and never seems to actually produce anything.

And you can repeat this process forever. Forever. It never ends.

The alternative is to draw a map and lead.

The Choice

You can either fit in or stand out. Not both.

You are either defending the status quo or challenging it. Playing defense and trying to keep everything "all right," or leading and provoking and striving to make everything better.

Either you are embracing the drama of your everyday life or you are seeing the world as it is. These are all choices; you can't have it both ways.

Someone will hire you because you fit the description, look right, have the right background, and don't ruffle feathers, or because you are a dream come true, an agent of change sure to make a difference. I don't think it's possible to make this point too clearly. Being slightly remarkable is a losing strategy. Blander than bland can work, and it has.

Indispensable linchpin works and it is the future. But the in-between spaces are scary.

Heads, You Win

Perhaps the biggest shift the new economy brings is self-determination. Access to capital and appropriate connections aren't nearly as essential as they were. Linchpins are made, not born.

There's no doubt that environment still plays a huge role. The right teacher or the right family support or the accidents of race or birth location are still significant factors. But the new rules mean that even if you've got all the right background, you won't make it unless you choose to.

These are internal choices, not external factors. How we respond to the opportunities and challenges of the outside world now determines how much the outside world values us. In this section I want to outline some of the roles the linchpin plays and how you can choose to play them.

Will Working More Hours Make You a Better Artist?

Does painting more pictures help? Writing more words? Inventing more inventions?

To a point.

But most of the time, that's not what we do. Most of the time, we're doing non-linchpin work, doing someone else's work instead of our art. That's fine, as long as there's a balance, as long as you leave enough time for the work that matters.

The resistance encourages you to avoid the work, and our society rewards busywork as well. Serious artists distinguish between the work and the stuff they have to do when they're not doing the work.

The Typical Transaction (and the Missing Arrow)

The typical transaction at work looks like this:

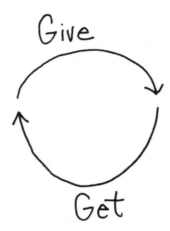

The boss gives you an assignment; you do the work. In return, she gives you money. It's an exchange, one not so different from shopping at the local store. You, the customer, are the boss. You exchange your money for an item on the shelf, and both sides win.

Of course, if the store charges more than the competition, you'll switch and buy from someone cheaper. As the boss, that's how you maximize what you get for your money. And the store? If they can find a customer willing to pay more for their product, they'll go ahead and sell it to someone else.

So, what's missing?

The gift.

If you give your boss the gift of art, insight, initiative, or connection, she's less likely to shop around every day looking to replace the commodity work you do, because the work you do isn't a commodity.

If the store you visit gives you the unmeasurable and unrequired gift of pleasant service, connection, respect, and joy, then you're a lot less likely to switch to the big-box store down the street to save a few dollars. You enjoy the gift, it means something to you, and you'd like to keep receiving it.

The missing arrow is the gift. The gift represents effort. Effort is separate from money, separate from the job description, separate from capitalism itself. Creating a career where you are seen as the indispensable linchpin may at first seem to be a selfish goal on your part, but you will achieve this goal by giving selfless gifts, and those benefit everyone.

More Cowbell

A concert isn't merely about the music, is it? And a restaurant isn't about the food. It's about joy and connection and excitement.

The funny thing is that learning how to add joy, create art, or contribute humanity is a lot easier than learning how to play the guitar. For some reason, we work on the technique before we worry about adding the joy.

If you're going to go to all the trouble of learning the song and performing it, then SING IT. Sing it loud and with feeling and like you mean it. Deliver it, don't just hand it over like a bank teller. When you answer the phone or greet me at your office or come to a meeting or write something, don't bother if all you're going to do is do it. Sing it or stay home.

If you get a chance, Google "More Cowbell" and you'll find what is certainly the most relevant *Saturday Night Live* skit of all time. There's a lonely cowbell player in Blue Öyster Cult, and every time he plays the cowbell, he feels horrible. He's standing out in a band that wants him to fit in. It takes a brilliant record producer to persuade him that if you're going to play the cowbell, *play the cowbell.*

Blogger Brian Clark explains that adding more cowbell is pretty much your only choice. Either that, or have no cowbell at all.

Return on Machines

Investors know what to look for: return on investment. For every dollar invested, they want to calculate how much money they can expect in return.

Most organizations focus on return on machines. I don't mean only big, noisy, industrial machines. I am talking about the infrastructure of the organization. They have a system, a factory, a set of desks or buildings or computers or Web sites, and the goal is to extract maximum value from the machines they've got.

The sales force exists to keep the machines busy. The IT department services the machines. The human resources department makes sure that the people staffing the machines (they are part of it, after all) are obedient, reliable, and cheap.

We see the machine in its goriest glory when we look at the meat processing industry. Workers are regularly abused, injured, and lied to. Cattle are pushed to be killed faster and with less waste. The goal is to improve the efficiency of any part of the "machine" and to decrease costs as much as possible. To do anything else means giving up profit at the superstore.

The slaughterhouse may not have many viable choices. The system these people work in has forced them to be the commodity processor of a commodity product.

But you don't have to work in a slaughterhouse.

Learning the Tools

I'm always amazed when I meet a writer who can't use a computer, or a lawyer who's uncomfortable with LexisNexis, or an executive who needs a corporate IT person to help him navigate an e-mail system. If you're a marketer unable to leverage your skills by using online tools, you're merely linked to the machines owned by the corporation. That's power they don't deserve.

The world just gave you control over the means of production. Not to master them is a sin.

On Strike for a Better Future

Jacqui Brown asked me what would have happened if, in 1990, the UAW had gone on strike against the auto companies.

What if, she wondered, the unions had gone on strike, not over wages or work rules but because the car companies weren't being innovative enough? What if they had walked out not over a contract dispute but because the industry refused to challenge the status quo and reinvent itself?

Hard to imagine, isn't it?

The work-hard mindset, combined with the us/them mindset, is so baked into the way that labor (that's most of us) deals with management (that's the boss) that it's inconceivable to us that organized labor would care enough about management's unwillingness to think differently that they would strike over it.

But what if they had? What if the culture of Detroit had been jolted twenty years ago and the parties involved had not set out to maximize return on machines but instead had focused on creating interactions and innovations that people would have chosen to pay for?

Obviously, it's too late to pull that off with the same power that it could have had then. But what about your boss or your industry? What happens when we acknowledge that the indispensable job is the only one worth doing, that the remarkable product is the only one worth paying extra for?

If your organization won't live without a map, can you change it? If you can't, should you leave?

A Timid Trapeze Artist Is a Dead Trapeze Artist

When big change hits, it is rarely gradual.

A hurricane hits but the levee holds.

Then another one hits and the levee holds.

There's no change from a normal day.

Then a big one hits and the levee breaks.

One day a system works; the next, it's underwater. The challenge here is that we can see the changes coming and we try to deal with them by making incremental changes, by being timid, by waiting to see what happens. So by the time what is going to happen happens, we're toast.

In the circus, the only way to make it as a trapeze artist is to leap. And what the linchpin who leads change is able to do is just that: leap.

When industries make transitions, 90 percent of the people squander their momentum, waste their resources, and grudgingly tiptoe from the perfect sector/job/market they were in and try to make their way over to the new opportunity. And along the way, those 90 percent are outfoxed, outgunned, and outwitted by the brave few.

This new American Dream I'm talking about, this revolution in relevance, in mattering, in interacting—there isn't room for everyone, not yet anyway. Instead, we'll keep slots open until we have enough indispensable people, until we have found the few people willing to abandon their résumés, throw out the rule book, and make a difference.

Then we'll get back to work.

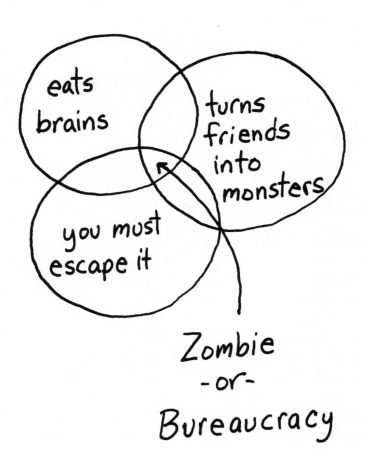

How Big Is Your Badge?

I gave a talk to one hundred top people at the Food and Drug Administration. If you think that the ideas in this book are only for small start-ups and that big companies are exempt, consider the vast bureaucracy that we call the Federal Government.

The best people in government are working desperately to find and challenge and leverage their linchpins. They understand that the FDA's slow-approval, bureaucratic, nongenomic map is long gone, that innovation is desperately needed and they have to hurry.

During the Q&A after my talk, an enforcement officer raised his hand and said, "They want us to invent a new future and to lead tribes and to make a difference, but we don't have any authority. I can't get anything done without authority."

This from a man who wears a uniform and carries a badge.

I said, "How much bigger do you need your badge to be?"

The fact is, a bigger badge isn't going to help at all. People aren't going to follow you because you order them to. They're not going to seek out a new path because you tell them that they must.

Linchpins don't need authority. It's not part of the deal. Authority matters only in the factory, not in your world.

Real change rarely comes from the front of the line. It happens from the middle or even the back. Real change happens when someone who cares steps up and takes what feels like a risk. People follow because they want to, not because you can order them to.

Does Your Job Match Your Passion?

Or does your passion match your job?

Conventional wisdom is that you should find a job that matches your passion. I think this is backwards.

I've argued repeatedly that your product should match your marketing, not the other way around, and the same inversion is true here. Transferring your passion to your job is far easier than finding a job that happens to match your passion.

Fit In or Stand Out

There are countless people waiting to tell you how to fit in, waiting to correct you, advise you, show you what you are doing wrong.

And no one pushing you to stand out.

If you add up all the books, scolds, back-benchers, bosses, teachers, parents, cops, co-workers, employees, religious zealots, politicians, and friends who can show you how to fit in just so, it's sort of overwhelming. It's clear to me that we're really good at establishing and reinforcing the status quo.

Fit in too much, though, and nothing much happens. Where are the self-appointed agitators and firebrands, the people who will egg you on and push you to stand for something?

They seem to be missing.

How Does a Linchpin Work?

In a world with only a few indispensable people, the linchpin has two elegant choices:

1. Hire plenty of factory workers. Scale like crazy. Take advantage of the fact that most people want a map, most people are willing to work cheaply, most people want to be the factory. You win because you extract the value of their labor, the labor they're surrendering too cheaply.

2. Find a boss who can't live without a linchpin. Find a boss who adequately values your scarcity and your contribution, who will reward you with freedom and respect. Do the work. Make a difference.

If you are not currently doing either of these, refuse to settle. You deserve better.

If Only . . .

Corporate coach Deanna Vogt challenged me to fill in the sentence, "I could be more creative if only . . ."

"If only" is a great way to eliminate your excuse du jour. "If only" is an obligator, because once you get rid of that item, you've got no excuse left, only the obligation.

I could see the situation more accurately if only . . .

I could lead this tribe if only . . .

I could find the bravery to do my art if only . . .

Nostalgia for the Future

For many of us, the happiest future is one that's precisely like the past, except a little better.

We all enjoy nostalgia (the real kind, nostalgia for the past). We gladly suffer from that bittersweet feeling we get about events that we loved, but can't relive. Nostalgia for the way we felt that day in high school, or for the bonhomie of a great team, or for a particular family event.

We'd love to do it again, but we can't.

Nostalgia for the future is that very same feeling about things that haven't happened yet. We are prepared for them to happen, but if something comes along to change our future, those things won't happen and we'll be disappointed.

If your company lays you off, you may very well get another job, but it won't be the job that one day was going to get you the promotion you were imagining that led to the event that you were hoping for in that office you were visualizing.

We're good at visualizing this future, and if we think it's not going to happen, we get nostalgic for it. This isn't positive visualization, it's attachment of the worst sort. We're attached to an outcome, often one we can't control.

If you had a chance to remake your life with a wish, what would you wish for? Would you leave behind your family, your town, your appearance? Most people would merely change the fabric on their sofa or make their job a little better (and their salary go up).

Some people, though, have an itch for a different future, one with radically different rules. Those people are emotionally connected to the sort of drive and visionary leadership that organizations look for in a linchpin. It's not a skill or even a talent. It's a choice.

You don't want your head of business development to have serious nostalgia for a particular future. If she does, she'll hold on to the deals and structures that make that future appear, and undervalue alternatives that could dramatically improve your organization, at the same time that her future vision is threatened.

The New York Times was offered a deal with Amazon during the 1990s. It would have transformed the economics of the paper and delivered billions of dollars in revenue over time. According to former CFO Diane Baker, senior management turned it down. They were worried that they would upset Barnes & Noble, which at the time was a big advertiser. Management had nostalgia for a future with steady increases in their current business, and felt threatened by a radical shift in that future.

The book publishing business is also run by people with this affliction. They love their industry, their product, their systems, and the joy it brings them. New technologies and business systems undermine that vision, and publishers often dismiss them because of simple nostalgia. The same thing happened to Kodak and to the big accounting firms.

The linchpin is able to invent a future, fall in love with it, live in it— and then abandon it on a moment's notice.

The Stressful Part Is the Hoping

Patients who were given colostomies (an operation in which a large portion of the colon is removed) were measured on their long-term happiness. The patients who were told that the situation was permanent, that they would need to live with a bag their entire lives, ended up being happier than those who were told that there was a chance they'd recover use of their colon.

The stressful part is the hoping. Hoping against hope that your plane will arrive, that you won't miss it, that your seat won't be given away, that you won't crash, that you'll land close to on time. Hoping that the surgery will turn out okay. Hoping that your boss won't yell at you. All of this is nerve-racking for many people.

And the reason is your nostalgia for the future. You've fallen in love with a described outcome, and at every stage along the way, it appears that hope and will and effort on your part might be able to maintain the future quo.

Madison House and Passion

Madison House is a Colorado-based music management and booking firm. They represent artists like Bill Kreutzmann, The String Cheese Incident, and Los Lobos.

As the music world comes crashing down, they are thriving. How'd they do that?

Because of people like Nadia Prescher. Nadia is one of the people who run the firm, and like her peers, she loves the music. She comes to the shows when she doesn't have to, works on details that aren't part of her job, and expends emotional labor because she can, not because she's told to.

Successful musicians have plenty of choices. If they pick Madison House, it's going to be because the people at the firm care enough to make a connection, not because they're the lowest-priced alternative. Every PR and professional service firm can learn from this. When your people do what they do because they love it, it works. Even if they're not as technically adept as the competition.

Be the Linchpin Once

If you can do it brilliantly once, just once, then of course you can do it again.

I'm not proposing you play a perfect round of golf or conduct a symphony. Instead, success lies in being generous or understanding someone or seeing a route that others don't see. You've done this already, done it brilliantly.

You've calmed yourself in the face of anxiety, or done something for no compensation, or solved a problem with an insight. Then, most of the time, the world steps in and relentlessly unteaches you how to do it again.

If you've done it once, you can do it again. Every day.

Ishita's Meditation

Ishita Gupta wrote,

Every day is a new chance to choose.

Choose to change your perspective.

Choose to flip the switch in your mind. Turn on the light and stop fretting about with insecurity and doubt.

Choose to do your work and be free of distraction.

Choose to see the best in someone, or choose to bring out the worst in them.

Choose to be a laser beam, with focused intention, or a scattered ray of light that doesn't do any good.

The power of choice is just that. Power. The only thing we have to do is remember that we control the harnessing of that power. We choose.

Don't let your circumstances or habits rule your choices today. Become a master of yourself and use your willpower to choose.

Linchpins Can't Merely Grind It Out

Most of what people do all day is roach stomping. The little tasks that distract us from the art of the work, that slow us down and wear us out.

The good news is that plenty of people are happy to stomp the roaches for you. Your job is to hire someone to clean your brushes, organize your papers, and clear the way. Your job is to make art the best you can, to change the status quo, and to become indispensable. If you burn out along the way, you're not doing anyone a favor.

It's not merely about hours worked. It never has been. Do the work and get whatever help you need to do it as well as you are able to.

Notice I used the word "merely." Linchpins often work a lot of hours. Nora Roberts writes three books a year, writing six hours a day, every day. She's putting in the hours, but doing something more. Hours aren't enough.

Corporations are tempted to squeeze as much apparent productivity as they can out of each employee. That's the factory mindset at work. If you work on an assembly line, of course it matters how many hours a day you stand there. This new model is very different. Ji Lee is a provocateur and artist famous for his street art. He also happens to work at Google. I have no doubt that he's added millions of dollars in value to the company through his orthogonal thinking and big ideas. And I also have no doubt that if he stopped doing his external projects and showed up at work more often, his productivity would plummet.

This Is What Hard Work Looks Like

No self-respecting salesperson complains about spending seven hours to fly to a prospect, give a twenty-minute pitch, and fly home.

No brave utility lineman complains about climbing a high-power tower to fix an insulator.

And no hardworking assembly-line worker hesitates about killing a hundred chickens an hour on the slaughterhouse assembly line.

That's because it's work. We're used to it and we know how to do it.

Yet the work of inventing, brainstorming, and overcoming the fear of shipping appears too difficult to bear. The work of getting over an emotional reaction, seeing a situation as it really is, and caring enough to provide a gift—that's beyond the pale.

Nothing about becoming indispensable is easy. If it's easy, it's already been done and it's no longer valuable.

What will make someone a linchpin is not a shortcut. It's the understanding of *which* hard work is worth doing. The only thing that separates great artists from mediocre ones is their ability to push through the dip. Some people decide that their art is important enough that they ought to overcome the resistance they face in doing their work. Those people become linchpins.

The Gifts That Matter

Dignity is more important than wealth. Everyone needs "enough." But once we have enough (and enough may be less than you think), what we crave and want is dignity. Given a choice between dignity and "more," most people choose dignity.

Respect matters. Respect in all things—for your employees, co-workers, and customers alike.

The ultimate gift you can give, the one that will repay you today and tomorrow and heal our world, is that gift. The gift of connection, of art, of love—of dignity.

Resilience

You will fail at this. Often.

Why is that a problem? In fact, this is a boon. It's a boon because when others fail to be remarkable or make a difference or share their art or have an impact, they will give up. But you won't, you'll persist, push-ing through the dip. Which means that few people will walk in the door with your background, experience, or persistence.

> If our young men miscarry in their first enterprises, they lose all heart. If the young merchant fails, men say he is ruined. If the fin-est genius studies at one of our colleges, and is not installed in an office within one year afterwards in the cities or suburbs of Boston or New York, it seems to his friends and to himself that he is right in being disheartened, and in complaining the rest of his life. A sturdy lad from New Hampshire or Vermont, who in turn tries all the professions, who teams it, farms it, peddles, keeps a school, preaches, edits a newspaper, goes to Congress, buys a township, and so forth, in successive years, and always, like a cat, falls on his feet, is worth a hundred of these city dolls. He walks abreast with his days, and feels no shame in not "studying a profession," for he does not postpone his life, but lives already. He has not one chance, but a hundred chances.

> —Ralph Waldo Emerson

Loyalty and Generosity to Yourself

How often do you beat yourself up? How often does the lizard brain set out to slow you down or wreck your career by highlighting the critics, the failures, the missteps? They get away with their cheap shots because you allow them to.

We're surrounded by people and organizations that demand our loyalty. Bosses, brands, and even politicians want fealty and obedience and patriotism. But what about you and your work? Doesn't it deserve at least as much?

The self-hating artist burns out. The hypercritical lizard brain will pick apart anything we do in order to preserve its sense of short-term safety. The alternative is to develop a sense of loyalty to your mission and generosity to your work.

I'm not proposing that you become immune to feedback. In fact, the most generous thing you can do is open yourself to the feedback that improves your art and helps it spread. Discerning the difference between feedback that helps and criticism that degrades, though, will take some time.

In the meantime, ease up on yourself. We need you.

THE CULTURE OF CONNECTION

The Linchpin Can't Succeed in Isolation

If you can't sell your ideas, your ideas go nowhere. And if you lie about your ideas, we will know and we'll reject them.

The Internet amplifies both of these traits.

The new media rewards ideas that resonate. It helps them spread. If your work persuades, you prosper.

And the new media punishes those who seek to mislead. We have ever more refined truth-telling cues, and if you don't believe in what you're doing, we'll know, and you will fail. Honest signals are the only signals that travel.

The Five Elements of Personality

Lexical analysis involves collating all the words a culture has to describe something and grouping them into fundamental pillars. In the case of personality, most psychologists agree that there are five traits that are essential in how people look at us: Openness, Conscientiousness, Extraversion, Agreeableness, and Emotional Stability.

Here's the thing: these are *also* the signs of the linchpin. Work, great work, has been transformed in just a hundred years from doing things that involve heavy lifting to leveraging and enhancing your personality. If you hope to succeed because you are able to connect and work with other people, then that will require you to improve your personality in each of these five elements.

Do you know someone who is more open to new ideas or more agreeable than you? More stable or extroverted? More conscientious? If so, then you better get moving. It's so easy to fall into the trap of focusing on using a spreadsheet or a time clock to measure your progress, but in fact, it's the investment you make in your interactions that will pay off.

Creating a Culture of Connection

Think about business-to-business sales. The key point of distinction between vendors calling on a company is rarely price. It's the perceived connection between the prospect and the organization.

Now, consider job satisfaction. The key point of distinction between places to work is rarely the work you'll be asking the employee to do. It's the perceived connection between the employee and the people she works with.

Thus, the individual in the organization who collects, connects, and nurtures relationships is indispensable. This isn't about recording the information in a database somewhere. This is about holding the relationships as sacred as they deserve to be.

Only a human being can nurture relationships. It has to be done with flair and transparency, and it can't be done from a script. The memories and connections and experiences of the person in the center of this culture are difficult to scale and hard to replace. Which makes this person indispensable. Not anyone who has that job—only the people who have that job and act like linchpins.

Return on Connection Investment

Two people work in an investment bank. One has an MBA in finance, with a focus on using the Black-Scholes asset pricing model to value options. He's a quant jock, and a pretty good one. The other has pushed hard to become adept at working with people, and as a result has personal relationships with twenty-seven of the bank's most important clients.

Guess which one adds more value and is more difficult to replace. . . .

The Black-Scholes model is important, but it's easy to outsource or to do with a computer. Sure, a world-class quant jock, one in a million, that guy you want to hold on to. But a pretty good one? I'll take the human being over the computer every time.

The Secret of Frank at Comcast

He's a real person.

That's the secret.

Frank Eliason has been featured on the front page of *The New York Times*, on television, and online about a million times. Frank is the online face of Comcast Cable, the occasionally loved, frequently hated cable behemoth.

Frank figured out that angry customers were often using Twitter to vent their rage about Comcast and their service or lack thereof.

One day, Frank tweeted back.

He showed up. Not because it was in the manual or because someone told him to, but because he wanted to help. It was a gift, not his job. Frank was honestly interested in connecting, and his generosity came through.

And you know what happened? The tweeters rejoiced. They were so stunned that a real person (with a name!) was listening that they instantly became fans. In less than a minute, they were converted from enemies and trolls into raving fans.

That's how desperately we want to be touched by another person. That's how much the gift of attention from a person means to us.

He's Good with People

Paul works at ConEd in New York and has been recently promoted.

Paul's team visits neighborhoods that need new gas lines. His team digs up the streets, shovels dirt, lays pipe, and keeps the system from falling apart. He's the young guy on the crew, but he makes more than most of the team.

That's because Paul is good with people. Paul is the guy who rings the doorbell, deals with angry neighbors, gets access to basements, replaces shrubs—stuff that is essential, but is improvised.

ConEd can easily replace the flagman and the guy who runs the backhoe. Even the pipe fitters do a job that can be outsourced. Paul, on the other hand, is the key man, the linchpin.

Why is "being good with people" so diminished as a competency? Is it because we can't easily measure and quantify it? I think it's an art, which means that the person who provides it is an artist.

Paul can't write a play, but he's still an artist, and he benefits from this attitude every day. The attitude of the artist.

What Moby Says About Art

Moby, multiplatinum recording artist with a great haircut, had this to say about art:

> Ideally, the market should accommodate art, art shouldn't accommodate the market . . . I know, it sounds idealistic. I had been trying to make myself happy and make radio happy and make the label happy and make the press happy . . . and it made me miserable.
>
> I also don't really aspire to selling too many records. See, my friends who are writers sell 20,000 books and they're happy. My friends who are theater directors sell 5,000 tickets during a run and they're happy. I like the idea of humble and reasonable metrics for determining the success of a record. And I like the idea of respecting the sacred bond that exists between musician and listener.

The irony of this statement is that this plan will probably lead to Moby's selling more records, not fewer.

The Problem with the Script

When your boss gives you a script to read, or when you crib something from a how-to book, it almost never works. That's because you're not telling the truth, you're not being human, and you're not being transparent.

You might be parroting the words from that negotiation book or the public-speaking training you went to, but every smart person you encounter knows that you're winging it or putting us on.

Virtually all of us make our living engaging directly with other people. When the interactions are genuine and transparent, they usually work. When they are artificial or manipulative, they fail.

The linchpin is coming from a posture of generosity; she's there to give a gift. If that's your intent, the words almost don't matter. What we'll perceive are your wishes, not the script.

This is why telemarketing has such a ridiculously low conversion rate. Why corporate blogs are so lame. Why frontline workers in the service business have such stress. We can sense it when you read the script because we're so good at finding the honest signals.

Honest Signals in Everyday Life

Sandy Pentland is a researcher and professor at MIT. His latest work involves the ways that humans figure out what is really happening around them. His new book, *Honest Signals*, is named after his term for information that flows back and forth between people.

Research has shown that we can easily distinguish hundreds or even thousands of microgestures. We know that people all over the world smile in similar ways that have nothing to do with culture and everything to do with neural programming.

Talking is more than words. Communicating is more than a speech. It may represent what the sender meant, but it might not.

Dialogue, the words on the page, the words we hear, by themselves have almost nothing to do with what we believe, how we feel, or how we respond. We can hear an announcement repeatedly and do nothing. The words aren't sufficient. On the other hand, we can watch a movie with no sound and understand precisely what's happening. We can read between the lines and understand exactly when a boss is lying to us and when someone is disrespecting us, regardless of the words being used.

Your wife opens her anniversary present and of course you know how she feels, long before she says a word. Her body language and breathing patterns and the way she looks at you communicate everything.

Pop photographer Jill Greenberg took a series of photos of gorgeous little kids, but she snapped the photos moments after she had ripped a lollipop out of their hands. I don't need dialogue to know what's happening in the photo. The honest signals are apparent. I can hear the wailing from a thousand miles away.

Pentland's research shows that speaking quickly after someone has addressed you has a fundamentally different impact from leaving room between the words and sentences. He has researched speed dating and other interactions and can now accurately predict the outcomes of interactions without hearing a word that is said.

Here's the key takeaway: dialogue is expensive. It takes an enormous amount of processing power to absorb all these signals, compose a response, and broadcast it back. Because interactions so overwhelm our processing ability, it's almost impossible to fake your intent. Sure, you can probably fake the words, but the rest of you will give yourself away. Yes, it's the lizard brain again. The fastest part of our brain is busy receiving and sending microsignals that may completely belie the words we're using.

When you are stressed out of your gourd, we can tell. When you're lying, we can tell. When you are in pain, we can tell. The signals are honest because we're not that good at lying.

This has huge implications for the linchpin.

Genuine Gifts

The only successful way to live in a world of honest signals is to give the genuine gift.

Genuine gifts, given with the right intent and a respectful posture, meet our sniff test. All our senses are on alert, and the giver passes the test. We believe.

Now that we believe, a different relationship can occur. One about "us," not just "you." But only if you cease to manipulate me and stop doing your job. Do your art instead.

Let me restate this because it's so important:

We have everything we need, so we're not buying commodities. We're not even buying products. We're buying relationships and stories and magic. Our business, our politicians, our friends—it's all the same; it's about figuring out whom we can trust and work with and who must be kept at bay.

Corporations tried to depersonalize all of those so they could lie to us, so they could package commodities, so they could scale without involving humans. And now they're out of steam. The corporatization is not working as well.

Since all you have to sell are relationships, you have to bypass the scam filters. You can certainly try to be the rational best-price, most-convenient alternative. But if you can't do that (and who can?), then the only path available to you is to change me, connect with me, or make a difference in my life.

Wal-Mart wins because it's cheap and close. Everyone else who wins must do it by being generous.

And for that, you must be an artist and you need to mean it.

The Placebo Effect

It's been demonstrated again and again that the placebo effect makes people get better. When a trusted doctor gives you medicine, odds are it will make you feel better (it may even cause you to *get* better), even if the medicine is only a sugar pill.

Honest signals are the explanation.

If the doctor truly believes, truly cares, and can see us for who we are, we can sense that. It doesn't matter what she says; it matters what else we pick up in our interactions with her. The words don't cure us; our beliefs do.

If the placebo effect is enough to cure cancer (and it can), then it can change your client's mind and dramatically shift the way people perceive your organization. The same autosuggestion that heals bodies also changes minds. The people you deal with make instant (and often permanent) decisions about people, products, and organizations. Humans are not rational computing machines—far from it.

The people you work with won't change if you don't believe. The communication of enthusiasm and connection and leadership starts with the gift you give, not with the manipulation you attempt.

Why Don't We Believe That Social Intelligence Makes a Difference?

If you made a list of the top ten things you'd have a new employee practice, where on the list would you put "be comfortable with other people," or "engage people in a way that makes them want to talk to you," or even "be persuasive"?

It's easy to take a development day to go to a conference that purports to teach you the latest techniques in chemical handling. Far more critical for the linchpin-in-training is figuring out how to project enthusiasm and get people to root for you. Dale Carnegie understood this, but the technocrats running your organization have forgotten it.

THE SEVEN ABILITIES
OF THE LINCHPIN

Is There a List?

Linchpins do two things for the organization. They exert emotional labor and they make a map. Those contributions take many forms. Here is one way to think about the list of what makes you indispensable:

1. Providing a unique interface between members of the organization
2. Delivering unique creativity
3. Managing a situation or organization of great complexity
4. Leading customers
5. Inspiring staff
6. Providing deep domain knowledge
7. Possessing a unique talent

A Unique Interface Between Members of the Organization

If your organization is a network (and it is), what holds that network together?

Is it just the salary and each person's fear of losing his job? If so, you've already lost.

In a story so good that it should be apocryphal, Zappos offers graduates of their two-week paid training school $2,000 if they will quit their new jobs. Why would Zappos offer to pay great people to quit? Tony Hsieh, CEO, does this because he wants to be sure that every person at the company is there for the right reasons, not because she's getting paid. If you're willing to leave for a few thousand bucks, good riddance.

In great organizations, there's a sense of mission. The tribe is racking up accomplishments, going somewhere. That mission doesn't happen accidentally. A linchpin helps lead, and she connects people in the organization, actively and with finesse. This takes emotional labor, and it can't be done by following the instructions in a manual.

The organization also includes its customers and prospects. That means that if you are the person who provides the bridge between the outside world and the company, you are in a critical position.

In most organizations, people do these jobs because they have to, and they do them to spec. But occasionally, you find someone who relishes the opportunity. Darienne Page is the first civilian you meet if you're called to a meeting with Barack Obama at the White House. As the official receptionist of the United States, she views her job as an opportunity to make a connection.

In the moments between your being checked through security and arriving at her tiny office, she'll have Googled you. She'll be ready with not just a warm welcome and a smile, but with relevant information you can chat about. She's looking forward to the engagement, it's a chance to perform, to do some art.

Certainly, the White House will function without Darienne Page. But by escalating the job above the manual, she changes it.

Delivering Unique Creativity

Three fairly simple words, very difficult to combine in a meaningful way. Let's go backwards:

Creativity is personal, original, unexpected, and useful.

Unique creativity requires domain knowledge, a position of trust, and the generosity to actually contribute. If you want to create a unique guitar riff, it sure helps if you've heard all the other guitar riffs on record. Unique implies that the creativity is focused and insightful.

Delivering unique creativity is hardest of all, because not only do you have to have insight, but you also need to be passionate enough to risk the rejection that delivering a solution can bring. You must ship.

The resistance, our fear of standing out, rears its ugly head every time we're on the hook for this sort of work. So we avoid the work. The sparse list of people willing (and able) to do this sort of work makes it particularly valuable.

Managing a Situation or Organization of Great Complexity

When the situation gets too complex, it's impossible to follow the manual, because there is no manual.

That's why linchpins are so valuable during times of great complexity (which is most of the time). Linchpins make their own maps, and thus allow the organization to navigate more quickly than it ever could if it had to wait for the paralyzed crowd to figure out what to do next.

When I used to help run a summer camp in Canada, the craziest day of the year was travel day. Hundreds of kids going to dozens of cities around the world, all at the same time.

We had buses and cars and planes to coordinate. Kids with passports, kids who forgot their passports. Parents on the phone, parents at the gate, and parents who forgot to show up.

Out of ninety staff members, only a dozen could be trusted to handle travel day. They were ambassadors, cut off from the king, making decisions on their own in a foreign land. The good ones were priceless.

All of our staff members were great, but most couldn't handle this task. It required mapmaking and clear judgment, and if you hadn't practiced either, it was hard to invent on the fly. This isn't a gift you're born with. It's a choice.

Leading Customers

As markets fragment and audiences spread, consumers are seeking connection more than ever. In short, we're looking for people to follow, and for others to join us as we do.

The traditional model of commerce is that a tiny group defines a product or a brand, and a team of people go sell it. It's a one-way transaction and it's static. Tide detergent is Tide detergent; take it or leave it.

The new model is interactive, fluid, and decentralized. That means that organizations need more than a tiny team. It means that every person who interacts with a consumer (or a business being sold to, or a donor to a nonprofit, or a voter) is doing marketing as leadership.

There's no script for leadership. There can't be.

Inspiring Staff

Organizations obey Newton's laws. A team at rest tends to stay at rest. Forward motion isn't the default state of any group of people, particularly groups with lots of people. Cynics and politics and coordination kick in and everything grinds to a halt.

In a factory, this isn't really a problem. The owner controls the boss who controls the foreman who controls the worker. It's a tightly linked chain, and things get done because there is cash to be made.

Most modern organizations are now far more amorphous than this. Responsibility isn't as clear, deliverables aren't as measurable, and goals aren't as cut and dried. So things slow down.

The linchpin changes that. Understanding that your job is to *make something happen* changes what you do all day. If you can only cajole, not force, if you can only lead, not push, then you make different choices.

You can't say, "Get more excited and insightful or you're fired." Actually, you can, but it won't work. The front-desk worker at a hotel who runs out in the middle of the night to buy gym shorts for a guest isn't doing it out of fear of being reprimanded. He does it because he was inspired to do so by a leader who wasn't even in the hotel when the clerk decided to contribute.

Providing Deep Domain Knowledge

Earlier, I argued that having deep domain knowledge by itself is rarely sufficient to becoming indispensable. Combining that knowledge with smart decisions and generous contributions, though, changes things.

Lester Wunderman knows quite a bit about direct marketing. In fact, he invented it. He helped create the American Express card and the Columbia Record Club. When Lester agreed to serve on the board of my Internet company in 1996, I was thrilled.

It turns out that we didn't learn a thing about the tactics of direct marketing from him. Instead, my team learned about decision making and strategy. We came to understand the big personalities in the industry as well as the motivations of many of our partners. Mentoring is rarely about the facts of the deal (the facts are easily found), but instead is a transfer of emotion and confidence. Lester had drawn a map once before and so he had the standing and authority to help us draw a new map.

Mapmakers often have the confidence to draw maps because they understand their subject so deeply.

Possessing a Unique Talent

When I was a kid, I loved the *Legion of Super-Heroes* and the *Justice League of America.* These were comics for slumming comic-book writers, fun and sort of stupid stories in which a whole bunch of superheroes would get together, hang out in the clubhouse, and then work together to destroy some sort of monster that any individual superhero could never have bested.

Anyway, near the beginning of most of these comics was a scene where a stranger would meet the team. Inevitably, the heroes would introduce themselves. Of course, Batman or Superman wouldn't need an introduction, but the lesser (lower-rent) heroes had to speak up and describe their superpowers.

"I'm the Wasp. I have the ability to shrink to a height of several centimeters, fly by means of insectoid wings, and fire energy blasts."

Some fancy marketers might call this a positioning statement or a unique selling proposition. Of course, it's not that. It's a superpower.

When you meet someone, you need to have a superpower. If you don't, you're just another handshake. It's not about touting yourself or coming on too strong. It's about making the introduction meaningful.

If I don't know your superpower, then I don't know how you can help me (or I can help you).

When I tell the superpower story to people, they seem to get it. But then I ask them their superpower, and they pick something that might be a power but it isn't really super. It's sort of an *average* power. "I'm pleasant and compliant" is the one we've been taught. Sorry, that's good, but it's not super.

If you want to be a linchpin, the power you bring to the table has to be very difficult to replace. Be bolder and think bigger. Nothing stopping you.

"Of course there is," some say. "I wasn't born with X-ray vision or even a lot of charisma for that matter." Awhile ago, I may have agreed with that—you needed talents and gifts to make a difference. But today there are so many ways to lead, so many things to do, so many opportunities to contribute that I don't buy it anymore.

This concept gets to the heart of the chasm we're facing. You want your pretty safe skill to be enough. Enough to make you valued, enough to make you fairly paid, enough to make your life stable. But it's not. It's not enough because in a very connected, very competitive marketplace, there are plenty of people with your pretty safe skill. The "super" part and the "power" part come not from something you're born with but from something you choose to do and, more important, from something you choose to give.

The Dip is about this very thing. If you're not the best in the world (the customer's world) at your unique talent, then it's not a unique talent, is it? Which means you have only two choices:

1. Develop the other attributes that make you a linchpin.

2. Get a lot better at your unique talent.

It's possible that no one ever pushed you to be brave enough to go this far out on a limb. Consider yourself pushed.

Compliance and Humility

At some level, all of us are virtuous, powerful, and wise. But none of these gifts works all the time. We'll stray from our principles, falter in our efforts, or make a bad decision now and then. Which is why humility is so important.

Humility is our antidote to what's inevitably not going to go according to plan. Humility permits us to approach a problem with kindness and not arrogance.

But humility is not the same as compliance. Humility doesn't mean meekness or fitting in at all costs. Compliance feels like a shortcut to humility because it permits us to deny responsibility for whatever goes wrong. But compliance deprives you of your superpower; it robs you of the chance to make something better.

The challenge, then, is to be the generous artist, but do it knowing that it just might not work. And that's okay.

WHEN IT DOESN'T WORK

What Do You Do When Your Art Doesn't Work?

What happens when the conversation doesn't happen, the product doesn't sell, the consumer is not delighted, your boss is not happy, and the people aren't moved?

Make more art.

It's the only choice, isn't it?

Give more gifts.

Learn from what you did and then do more.

The only alternative is to give up and to become an old-school cog. Which means failing. Trying and failing is better than merely failing, because trying makes you an artist and gives you the right to try again.

"My Boss Won't Let Me"

The single biggest objection to changing the way you approach your job is the certainty that your boss won't let you do anything but be a cog.

Nine times out of ten, this isn't true. One time out of ten, you should get a new job.

Let's take the rare case first.

If you actually work for an organization that insists you be medio-cre, that enforces conformity in all its employees, why stay? What are you building? The work can't possibly be enjoyable or challenging, your skills aren't increasing, and your value in the marketplace decreases each day you stay there. And if history is a guide, your job there isn't as stable as you think, because average companies making average products for average people are under huge strain.

Sure, it might be comfortable, and yes, you've been brainwashed into believing that this is what you're supposed to do, but no, it's not what you deserve.

The other case, though, is the common one. You *think* your boss won't let you, at the very same moment that your boss can't understand why you won't contribute more insight or enthusiasm. In most non-cog jobs, the boss's biggest lament is that her people won't step up and bring their authentic selves to work.

It's entirely true that your boss won't take the fall for you, won't stand up for you when you royally screw up without notice, and won't guarantee your success regardless of your behavior. If that's your definition of "my boss won't let me," then we have a semantic problem, not a management problem.

A cornerstone of your job is selling your boss on your plans, behaving in a way that gives her cover with *her* boss, being unpredictable in predictable ways. You can't go from being a junior account exec to flying the company's biggest client to Cannes in a private jet and expensing it a month later. You don't *start* with the confidence of the company; you earn it.

Pulitzer Prize Fighting: You Might Not Be Good Enough

You're gifted, but you might not be gifted at what you're doing right now.

You may have a remarkable idea, passion, insight, or enthusiasm. But the market might hate it. The technology might not work. Your craft might be lacking. If your play is boring, your painting is banal, or your interpersonal skills are flat, you might be doing the wrong task.

There's no guarantee that anyone who sets out to win a Pulitzer is going to win it. There's no guarantee that merely because you're passionate about Web design, your site is actually going to be popular.

The vivid truth is this: now that we have the freedom to create, we must embrace the fact that not all creations are equal, and some people aren't going to win.

That doesn't mean you're a loser. It might mean that you're making the wrong art, drawing the wrong map. If you're not winning as a stockbroker, perhaps your art lies somewhere else.

The challenge lies in knowing your market and yourself well enough to see the truth.

Maybe You Can't Get Paid for Doing Your Art

The thing is, it's far easier than ever before to surface your ideas. Far easier to have someone notice your interpersonal skills or your writing or your vision. Which means that people who might have hidden their talents are now finding them noticed.

That blog you've built, the one with a lot of traffic—perhaps it can't be monetized.

That nonprofit you work with, the one where you are able to change lives—perhaps turning it into a career will ruin it.

That passion you have for abstract painting—perhaps making your work commercial enough to sell will squeeze the joy out of it.

When what you do is what you love, you're able to invest more effort and care and time. That means you're more likely to win, to gain share, to profit. On the other hand, poets don't get paid. Even worse, poets who try to get paid end up writing jingles and failing and hating it at the same time.

Today, there are more ways than ever to share your talents and hobbies in public. And if you're driven, talented, and focused, you may discover that the market loves what you do. That people read your blog or click on your cartoons or listen to your MP3s. But, alas, that doesn't mean you can monetize it, quit your day job, and spend all day writing songs.

The pitfalls:

1. In order to monetize your work, you'll probably corrupt it, taking out the magic, in search of dollars;

   and

2. Attention doesn't always equal significant cash flow.

I think it makes sense to make your art your art, to give yourself over to it without regard for commerce.

Doing what you love is as important as ever, but if you're going to make a living at it, it helps to find a niche where money flows as a regular consequence of the success of your idea. Loving what you do is almost as important as doing what you love, especially if you need to make a living at it. Go find a job you can commit to, a career or a business you can fall in love with.

A friend who loved music, who wanted to spend his life doing it, got a job doing PR for a record label. He hated doing PR, and eventually realized that simply being in the record business didn't mean he had anything at all to do with music. Instead of finding a job he could love, he ended up being in proximity to, but nowhere involved with, something he cared about. I wish he had become a committed schoolteacher instead, spending every minute of his spare time making music and sharing it online for free. Instead, he's a frazzled publicity hound, working twice as many hours for less money and doing no music at all.

Maybe you can't make money doing what you love (at least what you love right now). But I bet you can figure out how to love what you do to make money (if you choose wisely).

Do your art. But don't wreck your art if it doesn't lend itself to paying the bills. That would be a tragedy.

(And the twist, because there is always a twist, is that as soon as you focus on your art and leave the money behind, you may discover that this focus turns out to be the secret of actually breaking through and making money.)

Calling Ellsworth Kelly

Here's an artist's dream:

The Art Institute of Chicago hires world-famous architect Renzo Piano to build an extension to their building. Together, they reach you on the phone by conference call. "Ellsworth, we'd like you to create a huge mural for our new museum. You can do what you want, call us when it's done, and we'll send a check today."

Artists want their bosses to act like this. And perhaps, when you're famous and eighty-six years old as Ellsworth is, it will happen. Until then, understand that your boss is unlikely to come through.

The system we work in is changing, but it's an evolutionary change, not a revolutionary one. Organizations rarely give linchpins all the support and encouragement they deserve. Which means that your efforts won't always get what they need to succeed.

There are two tactics that can help you if you're not Ellsworth Kelly:

1. Understand that there's a difference between the right answer and the answer you can sell. Too often, heretical ideas in organizations are shot down. They're not refused because they're wrong; they're refused because the person doing the selling doesn't have the stature or track record to sell it. Your boss has a worldview, too. When you propose something that triggers his resistance, what do you expect will happen?

2. Focus on making changes that work down, not up. Interacting with customers and employees is often easier than influencing bosses and investors. Over time, as you create an environment where your insight and generosity pay off, the people above you will notice, and you'll get more freedom and authority.

Don't ask your boss to run interference, cover for you, or take the blame. Instead, create moments where your boss can happily take credit. Once that cycle begins, you can be sure it will continue.

The Endless Giving Cycle of Art

When you talk to people who are committed to their art, what you'll discover is this: they never stop giving.

They don't give for a while, hoping to get, and then, once they cross a threshold, become takers. Instead, they have a posture of always giving. That's what they do, because they are artists, not cogs. They are linchpins, not replaceable employees.

What you're doing might not be working, and you might not be able to do what you're doing and get paid for it. But I am certain that if you give enough, to the right people in the right way, your gifts will be treasured and your journey will be rewarded. Even if that's not why you're doing it.

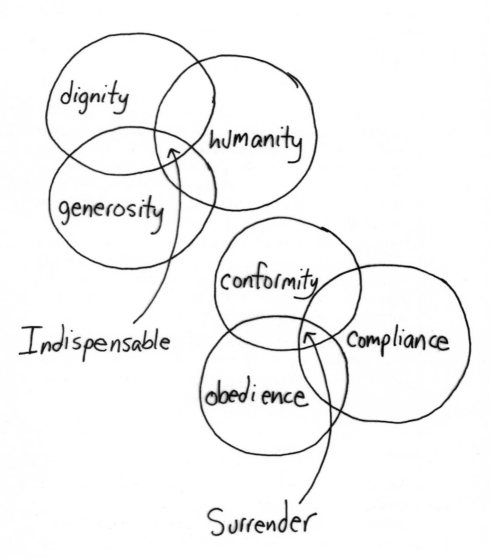

SUMMARY

The System Is Broken

I didn't set out to get you to quit your job or to persuade you to become an entrepreneur or merely to change the entire world.

All I wanted to do in this book was sell you on being the artist you already are. To make a difference. To stand for something. To get the respect and security you deserve.

If I've succeeded, then you now know that you have a gift to give, something you can do to change the world (or your part of it) for the better. I hope you'll do that, because we need you.

Sing in your own voice. Don't worry about finding inspiration. BEING POOR SUCKS. It comes eventually.

EVERYBODY HAS THEIR OWN PRIVATE MOUNT EVEREST THEY WERE PUT ON THIS EARTH TO CLIMB.

Start blogging. The choice of media is irrelevant. Write from the heart.

Don't try to stand out from the crowd; avoid crowds altogether. THE BEST WAY TO GET APPROVAL IS NOT TO NEED IT. SAVOR OBSCURITY WHILE IT LASTS.

You are responsible for your own experience. Power is never given. Nobody cares.

Whatever choice you make, The Devil gets his due eventually. Power is taken. Do it for yourself.

BEWARE OF TURNING HOBBIES INTO JOBS. Worrying about "Commercial vs. Artistic" is a complete waste of time.

Merit can be bought. Passion can't. When your dreams become reality, they are no longer your dreams.

allow your work to age with you. If you accept the pain, it cannot hurt you.

Keep your day job. Ignore everybody. Don't worry about finding inspiration. It comes eventually.

Remain frugal. Dying young is overrated.

If your biz plan depends on you suddenly being "discovered" by some big shot, your plan will probably fail.

NEVER COMPARE YOUR INSIDE WITH SOMEBODY ELSE'S OUTSIDE.

THE MOST IMPORTANT THING A CREATIVE PERSON CAN LEARN PROFESSIONALLY
IS WHERE TO DRAW THE RED LINE THAT SEPARATES WHAT YOU ARE WILLING TO DO, AND WHAT YOU ARE NOT.

Everyone is born creative; everyone is given a box of crayons in kindergarten.

Companies that squelch creativity can no longer compete with companies that champion creativity.

The hardest part of being creative is getting used to it.

Selling out is harder than it looks. You have to find your own schtick.

The world is changing AVOID THE WATERCOOLER GANG. Put the hours in.

Meaning Scales, People Don't. The more talented somebody is, the less they need the props.

@hugh

Will You Choose?

This is the scary part, of course. Your bluff is called. The barrier to success going forward isn't who you know or who your parents were or where you live.

There's no indication that you need to be born with a set of gifts or a world-class talent, either.

It's so easy to try to compromise, to do both, to fit in *and* stand out. Try for both, you may say. There lies failure. There's no room for compromise here, because those who are competing with you are specializing. They're going to obsess about either fitting in or standing out. *The act of deciding is the act of succeeding.*

The barrier to success is a choice. Up to you.

No Regrets

There's a popular brand of clothing with a huge slogan plastered on it: NO FEAR.

I think this motto is either disingenuous or stupid. Of course you should have fear. Riding a bike without a helmet may be fearless, but it's not smart. Lava surfing might be fearless, but it's not smart. Swallowing fire without training might be fearless as well, but we can all agree it's not smart either.

So, what's smart? Living life without regret.

Now that you know what to call the fear that has held you back all these years, what are you going to choose to do about the resistance? Now that you understand that society rewards you for standing out, for giving gifts, for making connections and being remarkable, what are you going to choose to do with that information?

You have a genius inside of you, a daemon with something to share with the world. Everyone does. Are you going to continue hiding it, holding it back, and settling for less than you deserve just because your lizard brain is afraid?

There lies regret.

Can You Change Everything?

You might not be as permanently stuck in a rut as you think. The rut you're in isn't permanent, nor is it perfect. There are certainly less perfect ruts, and there may be better ones as well. The certain thing is that you can change everything. If you choose to.

People have been brainwashing you into settling for a long time. It's easy to view your current situation as a box, a set of boundaries from which there is no escape. Of course you need to keep living your life the way you've been living it, because to do anything but that is too scary, too risky, too bold. Especially given your health, your family, the economy, your age, the neighborhood, your organization, your education, and your dreams. Everyone feels the same way.

And yet.

And yet every day a few people (more than a few people) change everything. You can do it. You can embrace a new path and take it. Don't settle. You're a genius and we need your contribution.

Do the work. Please.

Last Word

We can't profitably get more average.

We can't get more homogenized, more obedient, or cheaper. We can't get faster, either.

We've gone against our true nature and corporatized, anonymized, and dehumanized as many of our systems as we possibly can. Even health care is a system now, not a human interaction. We could probably go even further, actually, but I'm betting it won't be a fun or profitable journey.

If all mortgages are the same, of course they can be chopped up and remixed and resold. But that means all bankers and all homes are the same, and so are all homeowners. Which means the cheap ones or the profitable ones are all that matter.

If all online products at all online stores are the same, then of course I'll use a price-shopping Web site to find the cheapest product.

If all employees are nothing but a résumé, and résumés can be scanned, then why are we surprised that our computers end up finding us anonymous average people to fill our anonymous average jobs?

If every restaurant on the highway will give me precisely the same cheery service from the same robotic staff, at the same prices, then why does it matter where I stop?

Do we need to be flatter and smaller?

It's our desire to be treated like individuals that will end this cycle. Our passion for contribution and possibility, the passion we've drowned out in school and in the corporate world—that's the only way out.

Every successful organization is built around people. Humans who do art. People who interact with other people. Men and women who don't merely shuffle money, but interact, give gifts, and connect.

All these interactions are art. Art isn't only a painting; it's anything that changes someone for the better, any nonanonymous interaction that leads to a human (not simply a commercial) conclusion.

Art can't be bought and sold. It must contain an element that's a gift, something that brings the artist closer to the viewer, not something that insulates one from the other. So, we need to remember how to be artists.

Artists, at least the great ones, see the world more clearly than the rest of us. They have *prajna*, a sense of what actually is, not simply the artist's take on it. That honest sight allows them to see the future over the cloudy horizon. As our world changes faster and faster, it is these honest artists who will describe our future, and lead us there.

The only thing keeping you from being one of these artists is the resistance. The loud voice of the lizard brain telling you that you can't possibly do it, that you don't deserve it, that people will laugh at you. We don't have a talent shortage, we have a shipping shortage. Anyone who makes the choice to overcome the resistance and has the insight to make the right map can become a successful linchpin.

You can't fake it, though, because human beings are too talented at sensing when a gift is not a gift, when we're being played or manipulated. And sometimes, our art isn't enough. It's not enough to get us a sale or even a living. But we persist because making art is what we do.

The result of this art, these risks, the gifts, and the humanity coming together is both wonderful and ironic. The result of getting back in touch with our pre-commercial selves will actually create a post-commercial world that feeds us, enriches us, and gives us the stability we've been seeking for so long.

ACKNOWLEDGMENTS

Emily Boyd, Jon Dale, Rebecca Goldstein, Ishita Gupta, Clay Hebert, Alex Krupp, Susan Lewis, Al Pittampalli, Allan Young, Doug Rushkoff, Will Millberg, Hedy Kalikoff, Richard Weiss, Chris Anderson, Duncan Hines, Courtney Young, The Other Chris Anderson, Dave Balter, Greg Linn, Gary Gold, Blair Miller, Jim Leff, Todd Sattersten, Jack Covert, Lisa DiMona, Jacqueline Novogratz, Anne Jackson, Andy Sernovitz, Rajesh Setty, Micah Sifry, Megan Casey, Corey Brown, Gil to the rescue, Blake Schwendiman, Kimberly Dawn Wells, Stephanie Henry, Fred Wilson, Tony Hsieh, Guy Kawasaki, Michael Brooke, Charley Delana, Red Maxwell, Robert Shaps, Barbara Barry, Marina Sourbis, Derek Sivers, Micah Solomon, Joel Spolsky, Cory Doctorow, Henry Poydar, Zig Ziglar, Lynn Gordon, Sasha Dichter, Courtney Young, Allison McLean, Will Weisser, Adrian Zackheim, Michael Burke, Lisa Gansky, Barbara Johnson, David Evenchik, Shepard Fairey, Catherine E. Oliver. Courtney is listed twice because she was indispensable. Special thanks to people who read the acknowledgments. You know who you are. And to two linchpins: Admiral Barry Bronfin and Robert Leinwand.

Illustrations by Jessica Hagy and Hugh MacLeod. Google them, it's worth it.

And of course, Helene, Alex, and Mo. And my mom and dad, for pushing me to be an artist long before I realized what that meant.

BIBLIOGRAPHY

Here's a partial list, somewhat annotated, of some of the amazing books I had the pleasure to read while working on this book. To each author, "Thanks, and your work made a difference. I took a seed from your generous gift and grew it into something else, something that I hope will spread."

On Gifts and Art

The War of Art, by Steven Pressfield
In this short book, Steven sells a very important and simple idea. We are victims of the resistance, an almost irresistible force in our lizard brain that shouts down our genius and pushes us to fit in instead. Once you recognize the resistance and know its name, this knowledge will change you (for the better).

The Gift, by Lewis Hyde
Long, rich, and intricate, this book by poet Lewis Hyde takes us on a tour of gifts, art, poetry, commerce, and the history of the world. His understanding of how seemingly small decisions about things like usury changed our world forever is profound.

The Gift, by Marcel Mauss
Considered by many to be the breakthrough book on the economy of gifts. It's not a fun read, but stuff like this rarely is.

Art Is Work, by Milton Glaser
Milton Glaser does the work. Loudly and with pride and generosity, he has long led the way in thinking about the work and why it matters. This is mostly a portfolio, but the writing here will make you think.

Man on Wire, by Philippe Petit
Petit is an artist, someone living an adventure through his actions. His life is a gift to us, and this book, as much as the movie, will encourage and provoke you.

True and False, by David Mamet
Gripping, inspiring, and beyond-a-doubt true, this is not a book for actors, it is a book for everyone. Short and powerful.

On Sociology and Economics

The Lonely Crowd, by David Riesman, with Nathan Glazer and
    Reuel Denney
This is the best-selling sociology book ever, apparently. The key argument is that "fitting in" to a large group is a relatively new phenomenon, and it has changed the way human beings interact.

From the American System to Mass Production, 1800–1932,
    by David Hounshell
This is a powerful book, an extraordinary insight into the change from handmade to factory, from skilled craftsmen to cogs in a system. This really happened, and it happened to our great grandparents. The shifts were mammoth—in one two-year period, productivity at a Ford plant went up by more than five times.

The Power Elite, by C. Wright Mills
The first book to dive deep into the privileged class of American corporations and politics (largely the same group). Mills makes an overwhelming case that there was a caste system running our country, our schools, and our corporations. The vestiges still remain, but it's changing, in some places faster than others.

The American Myth of Success: From Horatio Alger to Norman Vincent Peale,
    by Richard Weiss
The evolution of our culture as seen through self-improvement books.

Weiss starts around the Civil War and goes up to the 1950s. What we read reflected who we were and where we were going.

The Managed Heart: Commercialization of Human Feeling,
    by Arlie Russell Hochschild
Hochschild was given significant access to stewardesses working at Delta Airlines in the 1960s. She chronicles the deadening pain they felt as they were forced to bring cheerfulness and emotion to work each day. I fundamentally disagree with her conclusion (that doing emotional labor is painful, not a privilege), but her work was considered a breakthrough at the time.

Stone Age Economics, by Marshall Sahlins
Despite the clever title, this is actually a book about how primitive cultures worked. One key takeaway is that hunter-gatherers were the idle rich. They worked about three hours a day and spent the rest of the day lolling about.

Life Inc.: How the World Became a Corporation and How to Take It Back,
    by Douglas Rushkoff
Doug is at the cutting edge of recognizing the collision between corporate values and human values. Most of this book is fairly pessimistic, and it argues that money has pushed people apart from each other. Harking back to Hyde's *The Gift* his point is that barter and community exchange do more than create commerce.

The Protestant Ethic and the Spirit of Capitalism, by Max Weber
Largely misunderstood, hard to read, and in some ways incorrect, it is still considered a giant achievement in sociology. Weber tries to understand the relationship between religious and commercial values, particularly as they led to the success of the United States.

The Communist Manifesto, by Karl Marx and Friedrich Engels
This book isn't about what you think it's about. And it's certainly not about the USSR. The key argument here is that small experiments in communism don't work, because they are corrupted by the temptation to defect and engage in trade with neighbors that exploit their workers (so you can benefit). Only worldwide revolution and grabbed power by farmers and factory workers can upend the unfair bargain that kings and capitalists have put in place. At one profound level they are right: as long as the

workers don't own the means of production, the exchange will be inherently unfair. A lot of what they pessimistically predicted has occurred to the workers at the bottom of the ladder.

The Wealth of Nations, by Adam Smith
There may be a reason to read this entire book, but if there is, it eludes me. The CliffsNotes are sufficient.

The Big Sort: Why the Clustering of Like-Minded America Is Tearing Us Apart, by Bill Bishop
Bill's key argument is that people choose to move to neighborhoods that vote and think the way they do. This is a logical outgrowth of the theories in *The Lonely Crowd*.

The Rise of the Creative Class: And How It's Transforming Work, Leisure, Community and Everyday Life, by Richard Florida
Richard has been in the forefront of doing scholarly work on how the workers who do own the means of production are changing our economy. Their decisions—from where they live to what they do—change the art created in our system and thus our lives as well.

The Trap: Selling Out to Stay Afloat in Winner-Take-All America, by Daniel Brook
A stunning indictment, very well researched, that shows how badly commodity workers are being hammered. If you're average, you're toast.

On Education

Weapons of Mass Instruction, by John Taylor Gatto
John Taylor Gatto is spitting mad, and no wonder. He has seen the worst our schools can do. He understands the history and is a victim of the bureaucracy. I wish every school board member, administrator, teacher, and parent could read a ten-page excerpt from this book. It's important.

Schooling in Capitalist America, by Samuel Bowles and Herbert Gintis
Thirty years old and loaded with accurate predictions about the future (and facts about our past).

Learning to Labor: How Working-Class Kids Get Working-Class Jobs, by Paul Willis

Ethnographic research from the 1970s that makes and proves a startling thesis: the very structure of school ends up establishing the "us and them" mentality that alienates most students from authority and sets them up to be unhappy wage slaves instead of productive leaders.

On Programming and Productivity

The Mythical Man-Month: Essays on Software Engineering,
    by Frederick P. Brooks, Jr.
Simple, useful analysis of a very complex topic, a new one for our age.

Software Project Survival Guide, by Steve McConnell
Steve's insights into thrashing are worth the entire price of his book.

Joel on Software, by Joel Spolsky
Joel is the best writer on managing brilliant people that I know of. Hands down.

Zen Habits, by Leo Babauta
Leo's productivity insights are scary in their simplicity and effectiveness.

On Science, Evolution, and the Brain

Ever Since Darwin: Reflections in Natural History, by Stephen Jay Gould
There are so many wonderful books about evolution, it's difficult to pick one. I picked this one because of the quote I grabbed, but I could have easily picked books by Dan Dennett and Matt Ridley.

Honest Signals: How They Shape Our World, by Alex (Sandy) Pentland
Pentland is a professor at MIT, and this is ostensibly a book about some amazing technology he's putting together that quietly measures the interactions people have all day when they're not remembering that the system is watching. What it's actually about, though, is the incredible power of nonverbal communication and tribal hierarchies in the way we interact.

Iconoclast: A Neuroscientist Reveals How to Think Differently, by Gregory Berns
Berns covers some of the same territory I do, but from a biological point of view. His take is that perception, fear, and networking are the three underlying neurological factors that lead some people to be original thinkers. It

was vindicating to read his book just as I finished mine, because his scientific data completely confirms the three pillars that I describe herein.

How We Decide, by Jonah Lehrer
This is a great introduction to the theories of the brain and our increasing understanding of how different parts of the brain work in concert to create outcomes we must live with. Lehrer references another great book, Antonio Damasio's *Descartes' Error.*

On Wisdom

Don't Bite the Hook: Finding Freedom from Anger, Resentment, and Other Destructive Emotions, by Pema Chödrön
Pema, a Buddhist nun who converted later in life from American roots, is my favorite teacher. She is able to simply and clearly connect with listeners and readers about a few powerful insights. In this book she talks about *shenpa*, the cycle of anxiety we buy into whenever confronted with a stressful situation.

Awakening the Buddha Within: Tibetan Wisdom for the Western World, by Lama Surya Das
There are countless books for Westerners in search of the simple insights of Buddhism. This book is quite detailed and serious.

Ignore Everybody: And 39 Other Keys to Creativity, by Hugh MacLeod
There are a million books about creativity. There are very few books that challenge the resistance so directly and effectively. This book eliminates the excuses that have been holding you back from being creative. It demands that you become an artist.

The Black Swan: The Impact of the Highly Improbable, by Nassim Nicholas Taleb
Taleb makes a compelling case that the predictable events that everyone knew were going to change everything are not predictable at all.

Peace Is Every Step: The Path of Mindfulness in Everyday Life, by Thich Nhat Hanh
This is not a book about religion. It's about seeing things as they are and finding things interesting instead of threatening. In a world without saber-toothed tigers, this turns out to be a productive approach.

On Overcoming Resistance and Getting Creative

Getting Things Done: The Art of Stress-Free Productivity, by David Allen

Presentation Zen: Simple Ideas on Presentation Design and Delivery,
    by Garr Reynolds

A Whack on the Side of the Head: How You Can Be More Creative,
    by Roger von Oech
All three of these books are classic collections of effective tactics. And none
of them will work until you make the choice to confront the resistance.

Key Blogs and Bloggers

Church of the Customer, Kevin Kelly, Joel on Software, Tom Asacker, Bob
Lefsetz, Clay Shirky, Jim Leff, Chris Anderson, David Meerman Scott,
Penelope Trunk, Tony Morgan, Brian Clark, Cory Doctorow, Indexed,
Stephen Johnson, Hugh MacLeod, The SAMBA blog, PSFK.

THE RES1STANCE

gifts
s
emotio
generous
Purple Cow
art indispe
honest signals
thrashing re
factory
lizard bra
cowbell
prajna
s